GOD'S WORD WRITTEN

GOD'S
WORD
WRITTEN

Essays on the Nature of
Biblical Revelation, Inspiration,
and Authority.

J.C. Wenger

HERALD PRESS
Scottdale, Pennsylvania
Kitchener, Ontario

GOD'S WORD WRITTEN
Copyright © 1966 by Herald Press, Scottdale, Pa. 15683
    Published simultaneously in Canada by Herald Press
    Kitchener, Ont. N2G 4M5
Library of Congress Catalog Card Number: 66-24292
International Standard Book Number: 0-8361-1900-2
Printed in the United States of America

15 14 13 12 11 10 9 8 7 6 5 4 3

To My Colleagues
On the Faculties of Goshen College
and the
Associated Mennonite Biblical Seminaries
and to
My Fellow Ministers in the Mennonite Church
I Respectfully Dedicate
This Book

CONTENTS

9 .... Preface

13 .... 1 The Word of God
32 .... 2 The Authority of Scripture
55 .... 3 The Meaning of Scripture
86 .... 4 A Christocentric Bible
106 .... 5 Transmission and Translation
139 .... An Attempt at a Synopsis

145 .... A Bibliography for Further Study
156 .... Index
166 .... The Author
167 .... The Conrad Grebel Lectures

PREFACE

In the providence of God it was my good fortune to be reared in a home and church where Christ was recognized as Lord, and where the Scriptures were read, believed, and obeyed. My undergraduate college training was taken at two Mennonite institutions, Eastern Mennonite College and Goshen College, in both of which the full inspiration, plenary authority, and trustworthiness of the Bible were taught without apology. My college Bible teachers were Harold S. Bender, Gustav H. Enss, Chester K. Lehman, and Edward Yoder. Following a BA degree from Goshen I enrolled at Westminster Theological Seminary in Philadelphia, where I sat under such revered scholars as Oswald T. Allis, R. B. Kuiper, J. Gresham Machen, Allan A. MacRae, John Murray, Ned B. Stonehouse, Cornelius Van Til, Paul Woolley, and Edward J. Young. At the University of Zürich I heard Fritz Blanke, Emil Brunner, Walter Gut, Ludwig Köhler, Werner G. Kümmel, Gottlob Schrenk, and Walter Zimmerli. At the University of Basel I attended the lectures of Karl Barth, Walter Eichrodt, and Adolf Köberle. Later I studied under C. M. Perry at the University of Chicago, and such professors as DeWitt H. Parker and Roy Wood Sellars at the University of Michigan. To all of these men I owe a debt of gratitude. Under Barth and Brunner I encountered the full force of the so-called Neoorthodoxy. Roy Wood Sellars was a religious humanist. DeWitt H. Parker was a philosophical theist. Harold S. Bender introduced me to Anabaptism. John Murray and Cornelius Van Til led me into the labors and joys of systematic theology. J. Gresham Machen challenged me with the vitality of evangelicalism. Fritz Blanke did more than teach me church history and historical theology; as a man of faith who loved the Lord he was also a man of deep influence on my Christian life.

In 1938 I began to teach at Goshen College and its Bible School (renamed the Biblical Seminary in 1946), particularly in Bible and theology, my special field of interest being historical theology. The academic year, 1964-65, I spent as a postdoctoral Visiting Fellow in Princeton Theological Seminary, auditing classes under Professors James Barr and D. L. Migliore, and preparing the lectures herewith presented in book form. From time to time I have also profited from discussions with a number of friends and colleagues, especially with my fellow instructors in the Associated Mennonite Biblical Seminaries, and with Myron S. Augsburger and Chester K. Lehman of Eastern Mennonite College. I owe a vast debt to the late Dean Harold S. Bender, at whose side I served for twenty-four years at Goshen. I am also most grateful to three scholars for reading the manuscript, and offering suggestions for its improvement: Professors F. F. Bruce of the Faculty of Theology, University of Manchester; Bruce M. Metzger of Princeton Theological Seminary; and Paul Woolley of Westminster Theological Seminary. It is also a pleasure to thank the members of the Conrad Grebel Lectureship Committee for their helpful suggestions: Paul Erb, Guy F. Hershberger, I. B. Horst, Nelson E. Kauffman, and G. G. Yoder. Needless to say, I alone am responsible for the point of view and the content of the book.

In writing these lectures I sought earnestly for the mind of Christ through a direct study of the Scriptures. I trust that He heard my prayers for the illumination of the Holy Spirit as I studied His Word. I have also endeavored to learn from writers of various shades of theological opinion, and from many periods of church history. I am impressed with the remarkable renaissance of theological research and writing which this generation is witnessing. In the research which preceded the writing of these lectures I was tantalized by the question attributed to the distinguished Swedish-born physiologist, Dr. Anton Carlson: "Vott iss tee effidence?" The reader will observe that my studies have brought me to a position which closely resembles that of the reformers, without, I hope, exposing me to the just charge of a wooden literalism or an anxious obscurantism. I confess that I have tried to make normative the view of Scripture which was held by the God-Man, Jesus Christ of Nazareth.

It was for me a distinct honor to be invited to prepare the Conrad Grebel Lectures for 1966. I took the responsibility seriously. I also tried to conform to the wish of the Conrad Grebel Lectureship Committee that the lectures be presented in a sufficiently simple form that common people could hear and read them with profit. I also tried to keep them from becoming excessively lengthy. There are therefore many questions of higher criticism which I did not deal with at all. But I did attempt to set forth and defend a stance toward such questions which I hope may be found to be sound.

May the Lord of the church, the God of all truth, be pleased to use this humble effort to encourage many of His saints to accept the divine-human book which we call the Holy Scriptures as in very truth, *God's Word Written.*

Goshen College Biblical Seminary   *—J. C. Wenger*
Goshen, Indiana
June 1, 1965

Preface to the Third Printing

The printing of a paperback edition of this volume has afforded me the welcome opportunity of making a few minor changes, correcting a few spellings, and adding a book or two to the bibliography.

The same perspective in relation to the doctrine of the Scripture which informed the book in the first place has been maintained.

Goshen Biblical Seminary   J. C. Wenger
3003 Benham Avenue
Elkhart, IN 46514
May 20, 1979

1
THE WORD OF GOD

Near the end of his lucid monograph, *The Idea of Revelation in Recent Thought,* the late John Baillie tells sympathetically of the complaint made by a certain man to Professor Baillie. The man lamented that in spite of the fact that we worship God, we put our trust in Him, we direct our prayers to Him, we bow down to Him, and we lift up our hearts to Him, yet He makes no response. It is, declared the man, "all so one-sided." That this man was in some measure not justified, Baillie is at some pains to show. And yet that man spoke for numberless millions of people who have yet to find a true word from God. This was that for which the Greek philosopher Plato sensed the need when he spoke of the possibility of finding a "sure word of God." John Wesley expressed this need vividly when he cried: "I want to know one thing—the way to heaven; how to land safe on that happy shore." And then he cried out ecstatically, "God Himself has condescended to teach the way; for this very end He came from heaven. He hath written it down in a book. O give me that book! At any price, give me the book of God" (Preface to *Standard Sermons,* edited by E. H. Sugden, London, 1746; Epworth Press Reprint, 1955, pp. 31, 32).

Has God Spoken?
Let us now take up that Book and look briefly in it. Does it really claim to present the Word of God? The answer is emphatically

affirmative. The Bible indicates that in very truth *God has spoken*. The God who spoke is the God who also acted. He is the God who by His spoken word brought into being the heavens and the earth. "He spake, and it was done," declared the psalmist. Psalm 33:9. And this declaration illustrates the dynamic character of God's Word: by His Word He effects whatever His intention may be. Even the creation of the universe was by His spoken word. The Bible itself begins with a majestic account of this creation. And majestic it surely is. Concerning Genesis 1 James Orr wrote: "However it got there, this chapter manifestly stands in its fit place as the introduction to all that follows. Where is there anything like it in all literature? There is nothing anywhere, in Babylonian legend or anywhere else"(*The Fundamentals*, VI, C. 1910, p, 85).

Genesis 1 is indeed a fitting introduction to the whole Bible, for it does not begin with a syllogism or with a reasoned defense of the existence of Deity. It begins with God in action. This is the God who created man "in his own image, in the image of God created he him" (Genesis 1:27). This is the personal God who came "walking in the garden" of Eden, "in the cool of the day"—only to find His creatures of the divine image in a wicked state of revolt. And right there in the Garden of Eden ("Pleasure") God manifested His infinite love and grace by announcing that one day the "Seed of the woman" would conquer the tempter. And this is the scarlet thread of redemption on which all the subsequent acts of God were hung, until Jesus Christ, of the seed of David, born of the Virgin Mary, died on the cross for the redemption of God's lost sons of Adam. As early as Genesis 6 we find this sovereign Creator and Redeemer-God making a gracious covenant with the faithful Noah and his family. With a remarkable compression of history, the account hurries on to the time of Abraham, something like two millennia before the Christian era. And with him God again graciously took the initiative in renewing this covenant of grace, a covenant with Abraham and his seed, promising him the land of Canaan, and a large progeny, and also stating obscurely that in Abraham's "Seed" all the nations of the earth would be blessed. Genesis 12 to 50 is devoted to the patriarchal narratives relating to Abraham, Isaac, Jacob, Joseph, and with Israel in Egypt, about to become slaves of the Pharaohs.

The second book of the Bible is devoted to the exodus of Israel from Egypt, her national redemption, when God brought His chosen people out of their bondage by His strong and mighty arm, under the leader whom He had caused to be marvelously prepared for his great role as lawgiver and prophet, the mighty Moses. Through the agency of Moses God once more in grace took the initiative and made a solemn covenant with His chosen people of Israel, giving them His holy law, and ratifying His holy covenant with blood. After the death of Moses, the Lord provided a leader in the person of Joshua who executed the initial conquest of Canaan. For several centuries the tribes of Israel lived in Canaan with only local judges, who also served as military deliverers, until the time of the prophet Samuel. Then at Israel's request, and by God's selection, Samuel anointed Saul as Israel's first national king. From him the throne passed to his son-in-law David, and from David to his son Solomon. After Solomon's death the kingdom was divided into the northern kingdom of Israel and the southern kingdom of Judah. Israel existed as a nation from about 931 B.C. to 722/21 B.C., after which her tribes were carried into Assyrian exile, never to return *en masse*. Judah continued as a nation from about 931 to 586 B.C., and was then carried into Babylonian captivity, only to return several generations later, a chastened people, now forever cured of all idolatrous tendencies. And finally, about 5 B.C., the Lord Jesus Christ was born, the long-awaited "Seed of the woman," who was destined to die for the sins of the world, to arise from the dead, and to establish the Christian Church by the gift of the Holy Spirit: all this about A.D. 30.

In the fullest sense the expression, *Word of God*, applies strictly to Jesus Christ, for He was the living embodiment of God. He was in His very person the incarnation of Deity. All that God is, Christ is. The incarnate Son of God is "the image of the invisible God" (Colossians 1:15); "all fulness" dwells in Him (Colossians 1:19). He is "the express image of [God's] person" (Hebrews 1:3).

God's Message Through the Prophets

In the Old Testament, however, when God chose to convey His message to selected recipients of His special revelation, the expression was commonly used: The *Word of Jahweh* [pronounced YAH-way and generally spelled Yahweh] came (literally "was") unto this person or that. The Word of Yahweh was in the primary sense not a written book but a living word received by the patriarch or prophet of the Lord. Thus in Genesis 15 "The Word of Yahweh came to Abram in a vision."

The prophet who was the chief recipient of Yahweh's Word was none other than Moses. Over seventy times the Scripture reports that "Yahweh spake unto Moses saying." (About ten times it is reported that He spake "unto Moses and Aaron.") The Scripture stresses how intimate the Lord was with Moses: with him Yahweh spake "face to face, as a man speaketh unto his friend" (Exodus 33:11). The expression, "Word of Yahweh," refers all through the Pentateuch to the living word received by Moses and other chosen servants of the Lord; it is not used of written scrolls.

The *second division* of the Hebrew Scriptures was known as the prophets, and consisted of two parts, the four books of the *former prophets* (Joshua, Judges, Samuel, and Kings) and—as the Jews counted—the four books of the *latter prophets* (Isaiah, Jeremiah, Ezekiel, and "The Twelve," *i.e.*, the twelve minor prophets). Once again the usage is uniform with the five books of the law: the Word of Yahweh designated the living message which God communicated to selected persons. Thus we read of Joshua being obedient to "the word of Yahweh which he commanded" him. Joshua 8:27. Likewise the children of Israel gave Joshua an inheritance in Canaan "according to the commandment of Yahweh" (19:50). When Samuel was a lad, "the word of Yahweh was rare" (I Samuel 3:1). Samuel later, as a prophet of the Lord, asked Saul to tarry with him in order that he might "hear the word of Elohim [God]" (9:27). Later the prophet rebuked the king for his disobedience to the Word of Yahweh (15:23), that is, the message which the Lord had delivered to Saul through His servant Samuel. In David's song of praise in II Samuel 22, and its parallel in Psalm 18, he proclaimed that "the word of

Yahweh is tried," that is, it proves to be true in the experience of His saints. Later we read that Abiathar was deposed according to the word which Yahweh had spoken of the house of Eli in Shiloh (I Kings 2:27), a word which the Lord had proclaimed to Eli through "a man of God," that is, a prophet. And in I Kings 12 we learn how the Word of God came to the prophet Shemaiah, forbidding Judah to go to war with Israel, and how Judah obeyed the Word of Yahweh. 12:24. The usage of the former prophets is exactly like that of the law: the Word of Yahweh means the message which He uttered through a chosen person. It is not spoken of a written scroll.

In the *latter prophets* (the books of the writing prophets, Isaiah through Malachi, less Daniel), the usage remains the same. Isaiah the son of Amoz received a message which he called upon the people to hearken to: "for Yahweh hath spoken" (1:2). He could therefore cry out: "Hear the word of Yahweh" (1:10). Again in Isaiah God speaks (40:1) and the prophet cries (40:8):

> The grass withereth,
> the flower fadeth:
> But the word of our God
> shall stand for ever.

That is, the message which the prophets deliver from the mouth of the Lord is utterly reliable. Jeremiah laments the spiritual hardness of hearing on the part of the Lord's people: "Behold, the word of Yahweh is unto them a reproach; they have no delight in it" (6:10). It should be noted that the difference between a true prophet of Yahweh and a false prophet was that the former truly received a word from Yahweh, while the latter claimed that Yahweh had given a message, when as a matter of actual fact, he had received nothing from Him. This differentiation is set forth in great fullness and clarity in Jeremiah 23. And so, one after another of Yahweh's prophets appeared in Israel, proclaiming courageously the Word of Yahweh which they had received from Him. "The word of Yahweh came expressly unto Ezekiel . . . in the land of the Chaldeans by the river Chebar" (1:3), to Hosea (1:1), to Joel (1:1), and so on. One of the worst judgments which Amos predicted was a famine, not of bread or water, "but of hearing the words of Yahweh" (8:11).

The usage of the phrase, "Word of Yahweh," remains the same in the Psalms and in the other books of the *third division* of the Hebrew Scriptures. The heavens were made by the Word of Yahweh. Psalm 33:6. Daniel 9:2 is somewhat unique, for the prophet writes of reading "in the books" how long the exile was to last, "according to the word of Yahweh to Jeremiah the prophet." In this case what was initially the spoken message delivered by the prophet had subsequently been recorded as indeed happened in the case of many of the oracles of Yahweh's prophets. I Chronicles reports that Saul died for disobeying the Word of Yahweh, that is, the word which Samuel spoke on behalf of Yahweh to the stubborn monarch. 10:13. Likewise the coronation of David was by the Word of Yahweh. 11: 3. After the tragic death of Uzzah, and King David had learned his lesson, the Levites bore the ark upon their shoulders "as Moses commanded according to the word of Yahweh" (15:15). A little later the Word of Yahweh came to the prophet Nathan in the night, "Go and tell David my servant, Thus saith Yahweh, Thou shalt not build me an house to dwell in . . ." (17:4). The many references in the Psalms to the precious character of God's Word must likewise refer primarily to the various promises, warnings, and words of comfort which God on different occasions brought to His people through His messengers, the prophets.

The Gospel of Christ

In the Scriptures of the New Testament the most common use of the phrase, "Word of God," is in the sense of the proclamation of the Gospel of Christ. James writes, for example, that God begat us "by the word of truth" (1:18)—that is, we responded to the invitation of the Gospel message, turned to Christ, and received the new birth. The "engrafted word" of which James speaks (1:21) refers to the way God stamps His Word in our hearts in the new birth. To be doers of the Word, not just hearers, means that we put to practice what we learn as the Lord's servants proclaim His will for us.

The usage of Paul is identical. The believers at Thessalonica "received the word in much affliction" (1:6); it was under conditions of stress and persecution that they heard the Gospel preached. And from them "sounded out the word of the Lord" (1:8), that is, they were faithful in proclaiming the Gospel. They themselves had heard from Paul "the word of God" (2:13). On the contrary, those who "corrupt the word of God" (II Corinthians 2:17) are those who do not proclaim the Gospel in its purity. Paul actually uses the full expression, "the word of the truth of the gospel" (Colossians 1:5). The expression, "the washing of water by the word" (Ephesians 5:26), refers to the spiritual cleansing which the acceptance of the Gospel brings. Calling the Word of God "the sword of the Spirit" (Ephesians 6:17) means that the Holy Spirit uses Gospel preaching to convict the unconverted of their need of Christ. And the writer of Hebrews speaks of those who have "tasted the good word of God," that is, who have had an experiential knowledge of the Christ who is offered in the preaching of the Gospel.

In the Synoptic Gospels and the Acts the *Word* also commonly means the message of the Gospel which the Lord's saints were proclaiming. "The sower soweth the word" (Mark 4:14). Believers experience persecution "because of the word" (Matthew 13:21). Many of those who "heard the word" became believers. Acts 4:4. The early Christians "spake the word of God with boldness" (Acts 4:31). The apostles thought it wrong to leave [the proclamation of] the Word of God to "serve tables" (Acts 6:2). In reporting how the church became increasingly active and effective in spreading the word of the Gospel, Luke says: "the word of God increased; and the number of the disciples multiplied in Jerusalem greatly" (Acts 6:7; *cf.* 17:13; 18:11).

In Peter's writings the usage is similar. Christians hear the word of the Gospel, accept the Christ there offered them, and thus are said to be "born again . . . by the word of God" (1:23). And this word of the Gospel "endureth for ever . . . the word which by [or, in] the gospel is preached unto you" (1:25).

John's writings sometimes employ the term *Word* in the Old Testament sense of a word from God, only in this case the Prophet was none other than the Son of God Himself: "I have given them thy word" (17:14). Similarly, "the word which ye hear is not mine, but the Father's which sent me" (14:24). The word which sanctified

the apostles was certainly this word from God which Jesus proclaimed. 17:17. As an aged patriarch, one who many decades earlier
had sat at the feet of the Son of God, the Apostle John calls Christ's
command to live in love, "the old commandment" (I John 2:7). John
was in exile on Patmos for his activity in proclaiming the Word of
God (Revelation 1:9), the saving Gospel of Christ. There John received the special revelation which we know as the Revelation; he
received it from an angel and "bare record of the word of God"
[which the angel] revealed to him. Revelation 1:1, 2. In the book
we learn of the saints who were put to death for "the word of God,"
for their activity in sharing the Gospel with others. 6:9; 20:4.

The Incarnate Son

But John has another, a unique, and a most important use of the
phrase, "Word of God." He applied this pregnant name to the incarnate Son of God. Hence he can write that "the Word" was in the
beginning with God, and that this "Word" was God. 1:1. Further,
this eternal "Word" became flesh, "and dwelt ['tabernacled']
among us . . . full of grace and truth" (1:14). John added his own
vivid memory: "And we beheld his glory, the glory as of the only
begotten of the Father." He described this incarnate Word in the
very beginning of his first epistle, stating how He who was "from the
beginning" had been in their midst: the apostles had seen and heard
Him, they had gazed upon Him—undoubtedly a reference to
watching Him as He ministered to them the Word of God in the
days of His flesh; indeed, they knew that this eternal Son of God had
really become flesh, for with their hands they had touched Him,
John declared. 1:1. And in the last book of the Bible, the Apocalypse—or, as the book names itself, *The Revelation of Jesus Christ*—
John described the visions he saw of the forces of evil and their power to harass the saints of God, a series of truly terrible and monstrous
scenes of persecution unto the death. But in the Revelation we are
also reminded of who it is who sits upon the throne and controls history, who it is who opens the seals, who pours out His vials [or
bowls] of wrath, and who has the keys of death and Hades. John
reports in chapter 19 a truly glorious sight. John saw heaven opened

and One sitting upon a white horse, and the first name of the con-
quering One of Revelation 19 is *Faithful and True*. His eyes were
like flames of fire, on His divine head were many crowns, and although His vesture had been dipped in blood [at Calvary] , He
was now waging a mighty spiritual conquest of mankind with the
"sword" of His mouth, the Gospel of the Crucified. His second name
was the one which is of interest to us in our study, *The Word of God:*
the One who expressed fully all that God is and all that He has to say
to the human race, the full revelation of the invisible God. Let phi-
losophers say what they will of the *deus absconditus*, the "hidden
God," John here portrays Him as the *deus revelatus*, the God who in
Christ has revealed Himself. And this revelatory Word of God is
none other, says John, than *King of kings and Lord of lords*—the
third name of our Lord in Revelation 19. So the Revelation portrays
Christ, as do many other portions of Scripture, in His threefold
office: a faithful high priest, a perfect prophet, and an omnipotent
king. He is a faithful priest to His failing saints, He is the true Word
of God who for our salvation became flesh and dwelt among us, and
He is the One with all authority in heaven and in earth, with a
name above every name both in this world and also in that which is
to come.

The Written Scriptures

Thus far we have seen that the predominant usage of the term
Word in Scripture referred first of all to the various messages which
God communicated to His people through His servants the prophets; second, it referred to the proclaimed message of the Gospel;
and third, to the personal Word of God, the incarnate Son of God.
There is still another sense to the phrase, *Word of God*, and this
fourth usage was instituted by the Lord Jesus. He referred to *the
written Scriptures* of the old covenant as the Word of God. Jesus
charged the Jews with ignoring *what Moses had written*, and heeding instead the oral tradition which had arisen in Israel, thus—said
Jesus—making void *the Word of God* "through your tradition"
(Mark 7:13). It is clear that our Lord is here referring to the sinful
disregard of the written Scriptures by His Jewish contemporaries,

and that He is calling the writings of Moses *the Word of God.* In a sense this is not in contrast with the first usage of the term *Word*— those messages which God communicated through the prophets— for it is clear that Christ regarded the instructions which Moses gave to Israel as having had their ultimate source in God. That which is new in the teaching of Christ is that the oral Word of God had now been committed to writing, and that the content of the books of the law may therefore properly also be called the Word of God. Christ was therefore saying: Let us test your practice, O Jews! Open the Word of God [Exodus 20:12] and see there what the duty of children is to their parents. Is it not to show them honor? Or turn to another portion of God's Word [Exodus 21:17] and see the consequences of rejecting one's parents. How can you Jews be so blind as to make void what God has spoken by your tradition which is not founded on God's Word? For Jesus, the spoken Word of God, had become "inscripturated." Indeed, what God originally spoke could in His day be known only by what had been written by those to "whom the word of God came" (John 10:35).

A second word from Christ on the subject of our investigation was spoken in connection with the charge that He was a blasphemer because He called Himself the Son of God. Christ's line of thought in His reply was that this was a strange argument indeed for a people who had available to them the written law of God. For in the holy Scriptures of Israel were not men of weighty office and dignity, such as judges, sometimes called "gods"? [See the Hebrew of Exodus 22:8, 9, 28.] Look in the holy law of God, said Jesus. Does it not call human beings who are serving as judges [study the context of Psalm 82:6] by the venerable term, *Elohim* ["gods"] ? Why then be offended by my claim to the Son of God? "If he called them gods, unto whom the word of God came, and the scripture cannot be broken; say ye of him, whom the Father hath sanctified, and sent into the world, Thou blasphemest; because I said, I am the Son of God" (John 10:35, 36)? Here Christ is drawing from the third division of the Hebrew canon, also calling it "law," and "Scripture," and its authors "them . . . unto whom the word of God came." And on top of it all, He remarked almost casually—so sure was He of His ground—"And the scripture cannot be broken." To those who accept Jesus as their divine Lord and infallible Teacher this is surely a strong testimony. Indeed, for disciples of Christ this evaluation of the Old Testament Scriptures by their Lord is nothing less than normative.

The Apostle Peter also refers to the written Scriptures of the Jews as possessing nothing less than divine authority. He refers to the awesome scene on the Mount of Transfiguration when with his own ears he heard the testimony of the Father: "This is my beloved Son, in whom I am well pleased." But, says Peter, we have an even greater authority than the testimony of one's own hearing; we have the written Scriptures of the prophets, the holy writings of our Jewish canon. These prophetic writings will illuminate this dark world until the glory of the *Parousia* breaks upon it! "We have also a more sure word of prophecy; whereunto ye do well that ye take heed, as unto a light that shineth in a dark place, until the day dawn, and the day star arise in your hearts" (II Peter 1:19). Peter continues by explaining why it is that the Holy Scriptures possess divine reliability. "Knowing this first, that no prophecy of Scripture is of any private interpretation" (1:20). Scripture did not originate in the private judgments and views of the writers of Scripture; they did not write down their private interpretations. "For the prophecy came not in old time by the will of man"—and here we give a more exact rendering of the Greek—"but men being borne along by the Holy Spirit spake from God" (1:21). It was the Holy Spirit whose "interpretations" the prophets wrote down, and it was this divine origin of the Scriptures which constituted them "a more sure word of prophecy." (Compare I Peter 1:10-12 and 1:25, RSV.)

We have already observed that in John 10 Jesus applied the lofty term *law* to a writing from the Book of Psalms—as He does also in John 15:25; and in exactly the same way Paul draws upon passages from all over the Old Testament—Psalms, Isaiah, Genesis—calling them all by the lofty term, "law." (See, for example, I Corinthians 14:21; Romans 3:19, and Galatians 4:21 f.) In precisely the same manner both Peter and Paul therefore draw upon the Old Testament writings as God's authoritative Scripture. We have already seen that Peter speaks of the "more sure word of prophecy" —or more literally, "the prophetic word made more sure"—and he turns right around and uses the phrase (in the Greek), "Every prophecy of scripture." Peter's phrase is remarkably similar to Paul's doctrine that "Every scripture is inspired [literally, breathed out] of God and profitable" (II Timothy 3:16), that is, its origin lies with God who "bore along" the writers of Scripture. The doctrine of inspiration held by evangelicals was not invented in the nineteenth century to refute Baur and Ritschl; it is based on the testimony of Christ and of His Spirit-led apostolic witnesses who wrote the books of the New Testament.

The author of Hebrews also speaks of the writings of the Old Testament as the Word of God. In chapter 4 he takes a text from Psalm 95:11:

Unto whom I sware in my wrath
that they should not enter
into my rest.

From this text the author of Hebrews makes a twofold point: (1) We enter at once into spiritual "rest" when we become believers; and (2) We must persevere in the way of faith if we wish to enter into the ultimate "rest," heaven, which corresponds in a sense to the earthly Canaan which so many unbelieving Israelites failed to reach. If we Christians have the wisdom we ought to possess, we will therefore take serious heed to Psalm 95 and make sure that we do not fall through unbelief like the Israelites of old. Rather we will see in the Scriptures how fatal unbelief [or disobedience] is in God's economy. We will give earnest heed to the warning of David. (In the Greek Old Testament Psalm 95 is entitled, "A Song of Praise, by David.") And what is this warning? The Scripture of Psalm 95 warns: "Today if ye will hear his voice, Harden not your hearts" (Greek Old Testament). And then the author of Hebrews gives us the foundation for taking this warning to heart: "For the word of God is [living] , and powerful, and sharper than any twoedged sword, piercing even to . . . the heart" (4:12). And he adds that we have additional reason to be on the alert spiritually: because the all-seeing eyes of God are also looking into our hearts. 4:13.

Our summary reveals then that in the Old Testament the Word of God meant the *message* which God's servants, the prophets, received from God and proclaimed to the people of Israel. In the New Testament it referred to the divine *message* of the Lord Jesus, to the word of the cross, the Gospel, as proclaimed by the early church; to the *written Old Testament*—the inscripturated Word of God; and supremely to the *Son of God Himself— the incarnate Word of God.*

How Did God Reveal?

Two questions yet call for a word of comment. The first question is, *How* did God reveal His Word to the prophets of old, to His servant Abraham; to His unique organ of revelation, Moses the lawgiver; and to the other prophets which followed? B. B. Warfield regarded the theophany [an experience of meeting God, such as Moses at the burning bush] as typical of patriarchal revelation. There were also dreams and visions, as Daniel's "deep sleep" until the Lord raised him up and communicated with him (8:18); Elisha asked for minstrel music to prepare him for the reception of God's Word (II Kings 3:15); the Lord "uncovered," or revealed to, the ear of Samuel . . . (I Samuel 9:15); *et cetera*. But generally the Bible simply indicates the *fact* of the communication, without specifying the *manner* of its reception. The mighty God who could create the heavens and the earth also proved Himself able to convey His message to His spokesmen, the prophets. Of the false prophets, God said (Jeremiah 23:21ff.):

> I have not sent these prophets,
> yet they ran:
> I have not spoken to them,
> yet they prophesied.

Then He adds:

> Do not I fill heaven and earth?
> saith the Lord.

> The prophet that hath a dream,
> let him tell a dream;

And he that hath my word,
let him speak my word faithfully.

Is not my word like as a fire?
saith the Lord;
And like a hammer that breaketh
the rock in pieces?

It must be clearly seen that, according to the Old Testament, God was both a God who *acted* for His people (redeeming them from Egypt, making a covenant with them, and manifesting His mighty hand on many occasions), and a God who communicated His holy and powerful *Word* to the prophets. And when the prophets came to the nation of Israel, the people whom God in His sovereign grace had chosen as His very own (Deuteronomy 7:6-8), they did not present their own private interpretation of the acts of God. God's acts were accompanied, either before or after, by His Word. His acts were not like a silent film which the prophets watched, and then added their own soundtrack. Rather, when God performed His redemptive acts for His elect people, He also revealed to the prophets the interpretation which they were to communicate to His people. Indeed—no matter how contrary this may be to some modern theories of revelation—the prophets testify regularly of the words or message which Yahweh caused them to *see*. "The vision of Isaiah the son of Amoz, which he saw concerning Judah . . ." (1:1); "The burden of Babylon, which Isaiah the son of Amoz did see" (13:1); "The words of Amos . . . which he saw concerning Israel" (1:1); "The vision of Obadiah. Thus saith the Lord Yahweh . . ." (1:1); "The word of Yahweh that came to Micah . . . which he saw . . ." (1:1); "The burden of Nineveh. The book of the vision of Nahum . . ." (1:1); "The burden which Habakkuk the prophet did see" (1:1).

There are now many authors, to be sure, who deny many of the acts of God as well as His revelation. One writer made the comment that the many accounts of people from Adam to Samuel "who heard with their own ears" the words of Yahweh, "spoken in person or by his 'angel,'" are simply "pious legends" which we may summarily dismiss. (R. H. Pfeiffer, *Introduction to the Old Testament*, Harper, 1948, p. 50.) But this rejection of divine revelation runs counter to the witness of the whole Bible, including the witness of our Lord Himself.

The Old Testament contains the record of the pathetic cry of King Zedekiah in his distress: "Is there any word from Yahweh" (Jeremiah 37:17)? The answer of God's servant Jeremiah was unequivocal: "There is!" One of the most impressive confirmations of this claim of the prophets occurs in a New Testament passage (Hebrews 1:1, 2) which may be set down as blank verse:

GOD
who at sundry times
and in divers manners
SPAKE
in time past
unto the fathers
by the prophets,
HATH
in these last days
SPOKEN
unto us
by his
SON.

Authorship and Date

The final question of our discussion may be difficult, but it is not as crucial as the one pertaining to the *fact* of divine revelation. It is the question of *when and by whom* the various books of the Scriptures were put into written form. For example, it is indicated a number of times in the Pentateuch that God told Moses to write down some item of history, such as the journeys of Israel, as well as God's law. And there is a uniform recognition from Joshua to Jesus that Moses was the one through whom God gave the law. Indeed, knowing what we do of Moses, his training, and his times, it seems unthinkable that he would not have been a man of letters. (Cf. Gleason L. Archer, Jr., *A Survey of O.T. Introduction, passim.*) On the other hand, it also appears that in the books of the law we have an occasional explanation or comment from a later hand. What about the account of Moses' death? Must we believe the views of those who have pictured Moses writing his own obituary with the tears streaming down his face?

Higher critical studies since 1750, especially in the nineteenth century, have radically reconstructed the picture which the Old Testament itself presents: namely that it was written in this order: (1) Law; (2) Prophets (Joshua to Malachi); and (3) Writings. This critical reconstruction was generally made by scholars who rejected miracles, who did not believe in predictive prophecy, and who thought that the faith of Israel was to be accounted for by a naturalistic theory of the evolution of religion. The fragmentation of Biblical books was carried to a ridiculous extreme. One writer, for example, cut Isaiah into fifty-five fragments and scattered them down through the centuries from the eighth to the second. (J. A. Bewer, *The Literature of the Old Testament*, Columbia University Press, Revised Edition, 1933, *passim.*) By the middle of the twentieth century, however, archaeology had done much to restore the confidence of many scholars in the basic trustworthiness of the Old Testament, and critical opinion had moved far in the direction of a more conservative position.

What stance may an evangelical Christian take in such matters of literary criticism on which there is not yet full consensus among Biblical scholars? Regardless of when the books of the Old Testament were written, and by whom (the former prophets—Joshua, Judges, Samuel, and Kings—are anonymous), our Lord and His apostles gave us the answer. They assured us in the strongest possible words that the books of the Old Testament may be regarded as God's Holy *Torah*, as the Scripture which "cannot be broken," as " [God-given] and [therefore] profitable for doctrine. . . . " The implication is clear. *The truth of God's Word does not depend upon who wrote it or when.* The evangelical scholar may therefore wait with poise for the achievement of greater consensus on questions of literary (higher) criticism. It is freely granted that a book may have been divided into two scrolls, as was done with Samuel,

Kings, Chronicles, and probably the original Ezra-Nehemiah. And how can we insist *a priori* that two or more scrolls could not have been combined into one manuscript like the Book of the Twelve [minor prophets] —or even two or three prophetical scrolls combined to make up the present Book of Isaiah?

But allowing for the possibility of such divisions or combinations—*should the evidence be adequate to establish them*—does not mean that the conservative scholar needs to accept every last critical theory which is advanced in a given generation. Rather, he will insist on the *evidence*. He will want to know what the theological assumptions are on which the theory is based. He will ask for proof. He will read carefully the literature which supports the proposed theory, and he will also study critically the literature which supports the more traditional view: knowing that there may be truth in both views. When a book by a scholar of great learning attacks the documentary hypothesis, for example, he will patiently examine it, asking if the author has made a genuine contribution to the literary criticism. (Incidentally, such a book is, *The Documentary Hypothesis and the Composition of the Pentateuch*, by Umberto Cassuto, Hebrew University of Jerusalem, distributed by the Oxford University Press, 1961. Another is the defense on critical grounds of the unity of Isaiah, *The Indivisible Isaiah*, by Rachel Margalioth, Yeshiva University Press, 1964.) In other words, the scholar worth his salt always reads books on literary criticism with a critical eye, regardless of whether a given author happens to agree or disagree with his own views. The answer to critical questions is scholarship of a high order, wedded, of course, to a vital faith in the God who speaks in His written Word. Higher criticism is obviously not trustworthy if it is wedded to naturalistic assumptions. (We will return to some sample problems of higher criticism in Lecture II.)

What stance therefore ought the Christian take on questions of literary criticism? Both the ordinary and the scholarly reader of the Bible will find many useful guidelines in the introductions to the several books prepared by Dr. Harold Lindsell in the *Harper Study Bible* (Harper & Row, 1964). The conservative scholar will not be tense and anxious, fearful for the fate of God's Word, for he knows that the truth has a way of overcoming error where there is the privilege of free discussion. And he knows that the truth and reliability of God's holy Word do not depend upon the higher critics and their conclusions. He will therefore be clear about his own theological assumptions, he will examine carefully the assumptions of the writers with whom he may be in disagreement, and he will humbly take note of what is being held by the ablest scholars in each field of inquiry. But he will certainly not accept uncritically every theory which happens to pass as the consensus of scholarly opinion at any given point. To accept as Gospel truth the so-called assured results of the latest scholarship in the past would have robbed the church of much precious truth, even of such pillars of the faith as the bodily resurrection of the Lord. The Christian scholar cannot be gullible, nor can he allow anybody to diminish for him the authority of God's Word. Karl Barth was certainly on solid ground when he insisted with his characteristic vigor that we cannot afford to slight the authority of any portion of God's Word. We dare not, says Barth, exalt the Synoptic Gospels as against John, nor stress the Gospels as opposed to the apostolic writings [epistles] . We must rather insist on *the full authority of the whole Word of God.* Its unity, declared Barth, with his fondness for illustrations, is like the seamless robe of Christ which may not be torn. (*Church Dogmatics*, I/2, p. 484 f.)

The most happy developments in Biblical scholarship since the two World Wars relate: (1) to an at least partial return to the authority of God's Word, (2) to a remarkable production of evangelical works in the field of Biblical introduction and theology, (3) to the encouraging flowering of Biblical theology in both Protestant and Catholic circles, and (4) to the gradual adoption of more conservative positions in higher critical circles, brought about at least in part by the remarkable findings of archaeology. William Foxwell Albright was able by the 1950's to report, for example, (1) that archaeology had demonstrated the antiquity of higher culture; (2) that the Wellhausian contempt for the accuracy of the patriarchal narratives was wholly wrong, for they reflect in very truth the precise conditions which archaeology shows obtained in the patriarchal age; and (3) that the old theory that the faith of Israel was the result of the evolution of religion has now been demonstrated to be "an impossibility." Indeed, thorough scholarship and archaeological evidence have brought the Albright school to a position which, in his own words, "strikingly resembles the orthodoxy of an earlier day" (Preface, *Stone Age to Christianity*, 1956; *The Bible After Twenty Years of Archaeology*, 1954, p. 550).

Again we must reiterate: *the authority of God's Word depends wholly upon God*, and not upon the ability of finite men to "demonstrate" its truth. To borrow another figure from Barth: the Bible as little needs our proof as the rainbow needs the earth to hold it up! (*Church Dogmatics*, I/1, p. 255.) And if a man is once convinced by the Holy Spirit that the authority of God is behind the Word, then *no question of higher criticism, or of history* (the date of the exodus, for example), *will be able to disturb his faith in the reliability of Scripture.* He will be able with Christianity's greatest theologian and writer, Paul, to speak of the Scriptures as the "oracles of God" (Romans 3:2). Phrases such as, "It stands written," and "As the Holy Ghost saith," will not offend him. For he is standing where Christ and His Spirit-directed apostles stood. Once again, as Barth put it, the statement, "The Bible is God's Word," is really "a confession of faith"; it is the confession which is made by the faith that it is God Himself who speaks "in the human word of the Bible" (*Church Dogmatics*, I/1, p. 123).

GOD HATH SPOKEN! Praise His holy name!

2
THE AUTHORITY OF SCRIPTURE

If what the Hebrew letter asserts is true, that God hath spoken by
the prophets and by His Son, and if all Scripture is God-given, then
*the authority of Scripture is the authority of its ultimate source, God
Himself.* Peter recognized this God-given character of the Hebrew
Scriptures when he testified that the Spirit of Christ indicated
through the prophets the sufferings of Christ and the glories to follow (thus the Greek in I Peter 1:11). For it is the character of all
Scripture not to have originated from man's unaided interpretation,
but being moved by God the prophets spoke forth from God. II Peter 1:20, 21. And the Lord Jesus indicated succinctly that Scripture
was incapable of being broken. John 10:35.

The Bible, Human and Divine

When one takes up the Bible, however, he discovers a paradoxical truth. The Bible contains many promises, warnings, and instructions from God. But it also records the sinful schemes of men, their
boastful words of unbelief, and even the sad story of many a major
act of sin and shame. Furthermore, the entire Scripture was written
in the living languages of Israel (mostly ancient Hebrew, with a
small portion in Aramaic, another Semitic tongue) and of the
Graeco-Roman world of the first century, A.D. (Koine Greek). So the
Word of God is recorded in man's languages, with all the limitations
which that places upon the Scripture. Furthermore, the Bible is not
only a Semitic book, for the most part; it is also an ancient book,

with the characteristics of ancient writings. For example, the speeches which the Bible records are certainly not generally full and verbatim accounts of the addresses made, but are good and true summaries of what was said. And when ancient writers quoted sources, they made no difference between direct and indirect quotation. (Note, for example, the way the Old Testament text is quoted in the New. The apostles sometimes made accurate translations from the Hebrew original, sometimes they simply gave the sense of the original, and most frequently they quoted from the Septuagint, whether or not the Greek version was a careful translation of the Hebrew text which we have.) Weights and measures and numbers are given in round figures as a general rule, and even such rough estimates of distance are given as "a sabbath day's journey." Often we find "about" this or that distance, "about" such and such a time, and the like. And even when the "about" is not stated, it is to be understood, for the Bible does not give data with the scientific precision of the twentieth century. Hence Solomon's temple laver was [about] thirty cubits in circumference and [about] ten cubits in diameter. II Chronicles 4:2. This is only one of the many aspects of the "humanness" of the Bible. (Had God desired to do so, He certainly could have had all observations and records made with infinite precision, but He chose to allow good and honest witnesses to put down their observations with the rough approximations of common people.) With conscious exaggeration the Book of Exodus reports that "all" the cattle of the Egyptians died—which meant simply that there was a fearful loss of cattle, not that none survived at all. And so the writer can tell us later in the chapter that the servants of Pharaoh who feared the word of Yahweh provided shelter for their cattle during the plague of hail. Exodus 9:6, 20.

The Bible, Religious Truth

It is worthy of careful notice that in general the Bible contains no revelations of what man can discover by scientific research—by the use, for example, of such refined instruments as the telescope and the microscope. For God spake through the prophets and through His Son, not to make human research unnecessary in any field of human knowledge, but to bring men into a saving relationship with Him through repentance and faith. God addresses man, not as a researching scientist, but as a lost sinner. He gave His holy law for a divine standard in matters of right and wrong, and He gave us the glad tidings of the Gospel of His Son to fill us with hope and peace through faith in His name. In a sense John spoke for all the apostles when he wrote near the close of his account of the marvelous deeds of the Lord Jesus:

These are written, that ye might believe that Jesus is
the Christ, the Son of God; and that believing ye might have
life through his name (John 20:31).

The account of the creation will serve to illustrate the religious concerns which motivated the writers of Scripture. Moses could have written all sorts of scientific data—if God had revealed it to him. Had a modern scientist attempted to write the first two chapters of Genesis, he would have begun with a statement of the age of the earth; but Moses says simply that "In the beginning God created the heavens and the earth." The scientist of today would attempt to give us some concept of the solar system, the size and mass of the sun, and of each of its planets and their moons, the size and shape of the planetary orbits, the location of the solar system in the "Milky Way," the number of such galaxies which God made, and the like. Coming to the earth, the scientist would have made a modern classification of the *flora* and *fauna* which God created, and so *ad infinitum*, writing everything from the standpoint of the findings and theories of the most modern learning, including, no doubt, some untrue hypotheses which later research would disprove! But this is not the character of Genesis. It was not written to make studies in biology, geology, and astronomy unnecessary. Rather, it gives a simple and straightforward account of how the God of Israel created all things by His all-powerful Word, of how His work was orderly and well arranged, and of how it all was "good," as the account states over and over. As to interest, the account is naturally geocentric, for man dwells on this sphere. As to emphasis, the account is theocentric, for it was God, and He alone, who acted on each of the six divine creative "days." *The language is that of ordinary people living in the ancient Near East:* vegetation and fruit trees; sun, moon, stars; flying creatures; huge marine forms and what one scholar has described as "the smaller fry" of the sea; wild beasts of the earth, and a broad term rendered "cattle" in the English version; and finally, the creatures which "glide" or crawl, probably reptiles in today's language. The account simply mentions the major forms of life known to common people in the early days of Israel, and reports that God created them all.

When one compares the Genesis account of the creation with such Babylonian myths as the *Enuma elish,* found at Assyrian Nineveh, there are superficial *similarities* of language and general scheme, such as the mention of the "deep," the creation of the earth and a covering for it, waters in the sky and on the earth, the establishment of a twelve-month year, the creation of man from divine materials, and so on. But the *differences* in the two accounts are even more striking. Genesis 1 is written in chaste and simple language, while the *Enuma elish* is mythological in form and polytheistic in outlook, beginning with the generation of the gods, and rehearsing their disharmony, strife, and crimes; the world is created in the fourth phase of the myth; and the long account (over 950 lines) ends in the praise of the god Marduk, not in the institution of the Lord's Sabbath. G. Ernest Wright is assuredly correct when he writes that it is "very confusing" to call the Biblical presentation a *myth,* for "nothing could be more different" than the total Biblical point of view and "polytheist mythology." (*Biblical Archaeology,* Philadelphia: The Westminster Press, Revised Edition, 1962, p. 104.)

The vivid and poetic Hebrew account of the creation fails to answer many of the questions with which scientists are concerned, for it is a truly religious account. Indeed, it has genuine theological depth. We gather from it how great the God of Israel must really be to have created by His Word all that exists, "the heavens and the earth." We learn that the Most High is sovereign over His creation, for He made it all. We see that man is a creature of dignity, for he was created in the image of God, and it was God who breathed into his nostrils the breath of life, making him an animate creature, "a living soul." We see portrayed in Genesis 1 a great personal God

who made everything "very good," and who is the kind of Deity
who has a plan for human history. (In contrast, the Babylonian
myths, with their polytheism and all sorts of imaginary details, are
grossly distorted and misleading.) It cannot be emphasized too
strongly *how utterly dependent we are upon the Scriptures* of the
Old and New Testaments for all that we know of God, of Jesus
Christ, and of the divine salvation which the Holy Spirit seeks to
bring to us. The Bible has a vastly higher function than to provide us
with the facts of mathematics or of science: it was all written by the
inspiration of God's Spirit to make us "wise unto salvation," even
the salvation "which is in Christ Jesus" (II Timothy 3:15).

It is difficult indeed to find a name for the type of literature
which we find in the early pages of Genesis. It is agreed on all hands
that the simple narratives there recorded were written to answer the
deepest questions which men face. What is the origin of matter, of
plants and animals, of man, and especially of human sin and
depravity? The term *legend* is not a satisfactory name, for it suggests
that the narratives are unrelated to real history, or at least that their
historicity is suspect. The Scandinavian term *saga* seems to be no
improvement over legend. *Parable* is usually used of a short story
designed to teach a truth which is not rooted in actual history. The
word *allegory* is generally used of an imaginary story to convey spiritual truth, again without particular relation to actual history: *Pilgrim's Progress* being an illustration. For lack of a better term some
Christian writers therefore strip from the word *myth* any association
with the idea of imaginary gods and goddesses and arbitrarily apply
it to the accounts in the early chapters of Genesis. The present writer
feels that this procedure is not a happy one, for it is difficult to use
words in other than their dictionary sense without conveying conno-
tations which are not intended. Could not a phrase be found to indicate less ambiguously the truth that in Genesis 1—3 we have *simple
narratives* which are not ends in themselves but which were intended to provide *true theological explanations* of man's deepest
questions? We have already observed that there are profound
differences between the Babylonian mythology and the Mosaic account. (And these differences are surely to be accounted for by the

ministry of the Holy Spirit to Moses as he wrote the illuminating accounts of the Creation and the Fall.) Moses did not write theology as such, nor did he write simple stories as such. What he wrote was a sort of hybrid between simple narratives and theological exposition. I would therefore suggest that we refer to the early chapters of the Bible as *theological narration*.

Rich Literary Variety

It should also be stressed that the Bible as a whole is not of one uniform literary form. It contains rather a vast array of literary types. We have poetry such as the Psalms and much of the prophets. We have allegories like the trees choosing a king. Judges 9. We have the many parables—dozens of them—spoken by our Lord (Matthew 13, for example). We have apocalyptic literature such as parts of Daniel and much of Revelation. We have much history in the Bible, particularly of the patriarchs Abraham, Isaac, and Jacob, and of the children of Israel, along with their relations with the surrounding nations; the four Gospel portraits of Christ and His ministry of teaching and good works; and the story of the early church and its missionary outreach (Acts). We have theological essays such as Hebrews. We have in a minor way even the attempt to deal with problems of theodicy (Habakkuk). We have the letters of Paul (arranged from Romans the longest to Philemon the shortest in our canon), of James, of Peter, of John, and of Jude: twenty of them exclusive of Hebrews, which is not really a letter. We have collections of wisdom, based on human observation (the Proverbs).

Perhaps the most enigmatical book in the Bible is Ecclesiastes. Both Jews and Christians have sometimes been puzzled as to how this book ever got into the sacred canon of the Old Testament. Possibly a brief analysis and interpretation may serve in part to cut the problem down to reasonable size. The book is actually a sort of debate between the voice of faith and that of pessimism. The spokesman for the latter point of view speaks eloquently of his efforts to find peace and abiding satisfaction through every form of human activity, from the sensual to the most refined. Neither bodily pleasure nor aesthetic stimulation, he tells us, is able to bring satisfaction to the human heart. All that man is capable of doing leads only to a feeling of emptiness and dissatisfaction. Nature too is involved in what appears to be a senseless cycle: the sun rises, and the sun sets; the wind blows north, then turns about and blows southward; the rivers forever run into the sea, only to repeat the cycle. Likewise man is involved in a meaningless round of striving. The generations come and go, and there is really "no new thing under the sun" (1:9). Trying to master "wisdom" [making collections of Proverbs, for example!] cannot satisfy the heart. Neither pleasure nor humor ("mirth") can bring real happiness. 2:1, 2. Great building plans, even when achieved, do not satisfy man's need, neither does horticulture, nor landscaping, nor wealth. "Behold, all was vanity and vexation of spirit" (2:11).

The gloom deepens as the writer proceeds. Not only is it impossible for human joys—wine to choirs—to bring ultimate satisfaction: the fact of human mortality, a truly crushing concept, must be faced. And what do we see in that area? All must die: wise man and fool (2:16); man and beast (3:19). And what follows death? Ah, there is the real problem for the man "under the sun." By empirical evidence, how can we know whether there is conscious existence after death? says the pessimist. For all we know, "the dead know not anything" (9:5). And yet this very book has the most beautiful description of old age and death (chapter 12) which is found anywhere in the Bible.

But there is also a firm voice which speaks up from time to time in Ecclesiastes, to strike down the overly pessimistic voice which is allowed so much freedom. This firm voice insists that *the simple joys* of food and drink, of toil and sleep, and of conjugal love *can be satisfying.* 2:24, 26; 3:12, 13; 4:6; 5:12; 8:12, 15; 9:7, 9; 11:6. And from time to time *the voice of faith in God also speaks.* 2:26; 3:10, 11, 13, 17; 5:1, 4, 7, 20; 8:2, 12, 15; 9:7; 11:9. But which voice is final? that of doubt and pessimism, or that of faith? The writer sums up the debate of his bosom thus:

> Let us hear the conclusion of the whole matter:
> Fear God,
> and keep his commandments:

for this is the whole duty of man.

For God shall bring every work into judgment,
   with every secret thing,
   whether it be good,
   or whether it be evil (12:13, 14).

The question is sometimes raised whether the story of Jonah is to be taken as literal history, or whether it was a sort of imaginary parable to correct the ultranationalism of Israel. In principle, we must of course admit the possibility of God employing just such a parabolic story. Yet the book itself certainly does not read like a parable; it purports rather to record how God dealt with a stubborn prophet who knew the will of God, and finally became willing to do it—only to enjoy incredible evangelistic success in the very nation which he inwardly hoped would be destroyed of God. James Orr admitted in 1910 that a prophet would indeed be free to employ a parable, but then added sagely, "One would like to feel surer that the application of the principle in this case is not simply a way of escaping from a felt difficulty in the contents of the Book" *(Revelation and Inspiration,* Scribner, 1910, p. 173).

Character of Bible History

It should also be freely admitted that there are problems connected with Biblical history. These problems may be minor—such as the length of the period of the judges (Acts 13:20), or the names of Esau's three wives, or the length of King Pekah's reign—or more significant, such as the date of Israel's exodus from Egypt. Whatever the solutions to these problems may be, one fact is certain: they are not a threat to the truth of Christianity. The need of historical research is no more ruled out by the truth of the Scriptures than is the need for scientific research. There is abundant evidence that the writers of Scripture were good and trustworthy men; but they were also children of their day and were not concerned to write "scientific" history. The best examples of this are not trivial items, such as those just referred to, but the very acts of God upon which the Christian faith rests! We cannot at this point determine the exact year of Christ's birth with certainty, nor can we be certain of the length of His public ministry. Indeed, even the year of His crucifixion cannot be fixed with absolute certainty. And this is true of most Biblical events. The Hebrew mind was concerned with the *fact* that God acted, and with the *meaning* of His acts, not with our ability to pinpoint them on a human calendar.

We have already noted that the apostolic writers generally quoted from the Septuagint, either verbatim or by giving its sense, even when the Septuagint was rather freely translated—and even when it deviated from the Hebrew text (that is, from the Hebrew text which we possess today). Similarly, the Gospel writers are not anxious about trying to make parallel accounts agree verbatim. They have no such wooden notions of truth as that it is dependent upon verbal identity. Each of the four evangelists feels free to tell his story from the sources he had, or as he remembered it. And there is no doubt about their having succeeded in giving a remarkably similar group of portraits of the Son of God in the days of His flesh—even though minor problems of Gospel harmony still remain. Indeed the very freedom of the Gospel writers is a major testimony to their integrity. Had their accounts always agreed verbatim when parallel, the very identity of the words would have aroused the suspicions of historians!

God's Saving Acts

The ultimate anchor of the evangelical in the matter of Biblical authority is *the position taken by Jesus Christ and His apostles*. James Orr penetrated to the heart of the matter when he stressed the fact that the Lord Jesus "intuitively perceived the inner connection of truth and history" (*Revelation and Inspiration*, p. 154). The Christian faith is not a matter of idealism, or of a *kerygma* which "works" whether or not the events of the story corresponded to actual events in space and time. "The truths of God's revelation [says Orr] . . . became the possession of mankind through *real* acts of God" (*Ibid.*, p. 154). God actually created the world. He truly called Abraham. He really commissioned Moses to lead Israel out of Egypt. He actually gave Israel His law and His holy covenant. He did entrust His servants, the prophets, with His Word. *He did send His*

Son into the world. And by a sin offering *the Lord Jesus did make atonement for the sins of the world. Christ did illuminate and guide the apostles as they wrote the Gospels and Epistles of the New Testament.* And the truths of Christianity are not endangered by the trivial problems of historical criticism which still remain. As Karl Barth put it: "We can and should cling to the written word . . ." (*Church Dogmatics*, I/2, p. 531). And we may not proudly set our selves up as judges of the Word, feeling competent to differentiate between the divine and the human elements of the Bible: "We are," declared Barth, "completely absolved from differentiating in the Bible between the divine and the human . . . cautiously choosing the former and scornfully rejecting the latter" (*Church Dogmatics*, I/2, p. 531). (It may be noted parenthetically that Barth is, however, sometimes a bit overzealous to recognize the humanness of the Word, even to the point of attributing error to the Biblical writings.) A safer guide here is Everett F. Harrison who seeks: (1) to accept the claim that the Bible is the inspired Word of God, and (2) to look with an open eye at the Scripture itself in the formulation of a theory as to what inspiration ensures and what it does not do. Harrison writes frankly and sanely: "We may have our own ideas as to how God should have inspired the Word, but it is more profitable to learn . . . how He has actually inspired it" (*Revelation and the Bible*, Baker, 1958, p. 249). And James Orr, who was less rigid in his doctrine of inerrancy than most neo-evangelicals, confessed with almost classic understatement: " . . . the Bible, impartially interpreted and judged, is free from demonstrable error in its statements, and harmonious in its teachings, to a degree that of itself creates an irresistible impression of a supernatural factor in its origin" (*Revelation and Inspiration*, p. 216). Karl Barth declared flatly: "Scripture is recognized as the Word of God by the fact that it *is* the Word of God" (*Church Dogmatics*, I/2, p. 537). This is, of course, a confession of faith, not the conclusion to a logical syllogism. And it is a confession born of the Holy Spirit, and confirmed in the life of the believer, as the Scriptures lead him to saving faith in the Lord Jesus Christ.

The Bible's Trustworthiness

It is highly important that this study of the authority of the
Word be approached from the standpoint of the Christian faith. And
how does a given person become a believer? The usual pattern is for
him to grow up in a Christian home, and to attend the services of the
Christian Church where the Word of God is read and expounded.
And although the preacher is not infallible, nor is the church itself
infallible in its teaching office, the Holy Spirit is pleased to honor the
reading and exposition of the word of Scripture, and to use it to
bring conviction for sin to the heart of the listener. And if he will
hearken to the inner promptings of the Holy Spirit, he will come to
the point of repentance from sin, and to the surrender of faith—faith
in the Lord Jesus Christ, the One to whom all the Scriptures point.
The convert does not come as a proud intellectual who has found
Christian theism superior to all rival systems of thought (although
this is indeed the case). He comes rather as a penitent seeker who
has been awakened to his need by the powerful and discerning
Word of God. *He has discovered what the real nature of Biblical
authority is. It is to witness to Christ and His salvation.* And that
witness embraces in a broad sweep the whole corpus of the Scriptures from the creation of all things by the "Word," the Christ of
God, to His personal return in glory on the Last Day. This is the
sweep from Genesis 1 to Revelation 22. And God is pleased to invest
His authority *only in this written Word as illuminated in human
hearts by His Spirit.* Neither the individual Christian, nor the clergy
individually or collectively, nor the whole church, may claim the
authority which God has been pleased to invest in the Holy Scriptures. The church must, thunders Barth, "ascribe direct absolute
and material authority only to Holy Scriptures," and he adds, "not
to anything else, not even to itself" (*Church Dogmatics*, I/2, p. 546).

In matters of human history and observation the Bible is truly
human, for it records events as honest observers saw them, not with
the infinite precision which would have characterized the events had
they been recorded as observed through the eyes of God. The central
concern of the Bible is not to give scientific classifications of animals—and therefore it is not surprising to find bats associated with

birds in the Old Testament, for the perfectly natural reason that they have wings and fly! Leviticus 11:13-19. And if Bible scholars are correct in identifying the Hebrew noun, *shaphan*, with the rock badger ("coney" in Leviticus 11:5 of the King James Version), the animal simulates the chewing of the cud, but does not really have the stomach of a ruminant. God allowed the various animals to be classified as to characteristics *as observed by common people*—not as classified by the Swedish scientist, Carl von Linne ("Linnaeus") of the eighteenth century! Once again we must insist that Biblical authority is in no way diminished because it looks at the world through the eyes of prophets and apostles, rather than those of a Linnaeus or an Einstein. And so we will never find the Einstein formula, $E = mc^2$ (Energy equals mass multiplied by the square of the speed of light), in the Scriptures, neither plainly nor in allegorical form! We go to science for relatively accurate information about this world. And we go to the Bible as the Salvation Book, the books of the Old Testament announcing the future coming of the Saviour, and the books of the New Testament witnessing to His having come and accomplished our redemption.

On the other hand, it must not be said that the Bible contains the testimony of unreliable witnesses. *The Bible is wholly true when read honestly for the purposes intended by God. In earthly matters it has the kind of reliability which would be demanded of honest witnesses in a court of law* (*cf.* the phrase of Gleason L. Archer, Jr., *A Survey of O.T. Introduction*, Moody Press, 1964, "according to the laws of legal evidence," p. 26). This leaves open to research the question of what divine inspiration did if a writer of Scripture was copying from a source which, although generally reliable, may have contained copyists' or other mistakes. Matthew Henry thought that such trivial discrepancies could be acknowledged without any embarrassment, and he was perhaps correct in this position. It must be emphasized again that the evangelical believer, although holding to the trustworthiness of Scripture, and accepting firmly its full reliability and its normative character for faith and life, does not set up *a priori* demands as to what inspiration shall or shall not allow. Such presumption would be crass human arrogance. Rather, he accepts wholeheartedly the full spiritual reliability of the written Word of God, and he carefully and patiently examines the evidence to determine what inspiration did or did not involve in such nonessential matters as we have been discussing.

No sixteenth-century scholar held to a higher view of inspiration than did John Calvin, as John Murray has recently shown. (*Calvin on Scripture and Divine Sovereignty*, Baker Book House, 1960.) Indeed Calvin frequently used that unspeakable word, "dictation" [by the Holy Spirit] , to express his high doctrine of inspiration! (He did admit differences of human style on the part of Biblical writers, however.) Again and again Calvin expresses his full confidence in the authority of the written Word. Indeed, his views have been described as the "rigidly orthodox verbal type of inspiration" (Kenneth S. Kantzer in Walvoord, *Inspiration and Interpretation*, Eerdmans, 1957, p. 137). And Calvin's disciple Murray holds equally firmly to the full inspiration and authority of the Scriptures. Yet when Calvin came across what seemed to be a minor discrepancy in the Scriptures, he was not disturbed—nor did he abandon his high view of the authority of the Bible. In commenting on Matthew 27:9, which purports to quote Jeremiah—when as a matter of fact the quotation is taken from Zechariah 11—Calvin simply acknowledges that he does not know how the name Jeremiah got into the text. Hebrews 11:21 poses another question. Should the last word of the verse be read as *staff* (as in the Greek of Hebrews) or as *bed* (as in the Masoretic text of Genesis 47:31)? Calvin observed that the apostolic writers were "not so scrupulous in this respect." He asserted, correctly of course, that the main point was "that Jacob worshiped." (The real explanation in this case is that the writer to the Hebrews simply followed the Greek Old Testament, rather than the Hebrew vocalization with which we are now familiar. As a matter of fact, the consonants were the same: whether one reads *bed* or *staff*, depends—as Professor Murray notes—on the vowels which are read with the consonants of the text.) But Calvin's words surely indicate that in spite of his "dictation" theory of inspiration, he was flexible enough to face up to the phenomena of Scripture without embarrassment or anxiety. He was quite ready to admit that the apostles sometimes put a rather surprising interpretation on an Old Testament quotation; in commenting on Paul's quotation in Romans 10:6 Calvin remarks that the quotation may appear to be "improperly twisted" by Paul, and in Ephesians 4:8 Paul seems to have "departed not a little" from the sense of the Old Testament passage. (See further in Murray, *op. cit.*, p. 25.) Yet Calvin always insisted vigorously that Moses and the prophets "spoke by divine impulse," conveying the message of God so accurately that "it was the mouth of the Lord that spoke"; and since the Scripture truly proceeds from God, it "has nothing of man mixed with it" (Murray, *op. cit.*, p. 18.)

The same high view of Scripture was taught by Martin Luther, and he could be just as paradoxical as Calvin in acknowledging the puzzling phenomena of Scripture, without being troubled by such phenomena—trivial as they are to all who do not hold to an overly rigid theory of inspiration. (It should be noted that the problem of the reinterpretation of the Old Testament passages in the New is far less acute if one takes into account the fact that the apostles often use the Old Testament "illustratively," rather than in the sense of full demonstration or proof. The point the apostle is making is often simply *clothed in Old Testament language*, even though it may differ somewhat from the apparent meaning of the language in its Old Testament context.)

If one may venture to suggest a crude comparison, the Scriptures are in some respects like a map made by a good and honest man, but without the benefit of a surveyor and an English teacher. The map might have a few hard words spelled wrongly (as the Hebrew tongue modified the name of Tiglath-pileser to Tilgath-pilneser in I Chronicles 5:6), and the distances from one town to the next might be only a rough approximation. Yet a total stranger, with the aid of the simple map, could find his way directly to his goal! Thus it is with the Scriptures. The language may at times be peasant-like in its lack of polish (for example, the deliberately ungrammatical *ho ēn* in Revelation 1:8), and yet he who will follow this Book, humble as parts of it may appear to the sophisticated of the world, will surely find his way to the Saviour. And it must also be emphasized that the Scriptures in themselves do not and cannot confer eternal life. Eternal life is to be found only in the Son of God, a divine gift to those who make the surrender of faith and who accept Jesus Christ as Saviour and Lord. Christ had to rebuke this very error in the unbelieving Jews—who made of the Scriptures an end in themselves: "[Ye] search the scriptures; for in them ye think ye have eternal life: and they are they which testify of me. And ye will not come to me, that ye might have life" (John 5:39, 40).

If we may tarry with the map illustration a bit longer: It would be possible to print the map on vellum, using colors of purple and gold. One could frame the map, treat it as a holy object, constantly speak of its authority and reliability, and so on. Yet maps are not ends in themselves. They are to be used as guides in going to a chosen destination. Just so it is with the Scriptures. If we do not use the Scriptures for their divinely intended purpose, to claim the blessings of the saving Gospel of Jesus Christ, to actually come to the Saviour and receive life in Him, we will not have discovered their true significance, nor understood the nature of their authority.*For the authority of Scripture is geared to its being the "Salvation Book,"* that is, the Book upon which men may rely to guide their steps to the Saviour.

Acknowledging that the authority of the Bible is related·to its central soteriological purpose is not a clever way to get around the nonscientific character of the Bible. (However, it must be acknowledged that it is nothing short of miraculous the way the Bible avoids the errors of all eras of its writing.) Refusing to "hunt" for scientific "revelations" in the Scripture is in very truth simply being honest in our use of it. All the statements of Scripture relating to its nature and authority point to its role as the inspired Guide to our Lord and Saviour Jesus Christ. To try to find all sorts of anticipations of modern scientific discoveries in the Scriptures is to distort and misuse the "Oracles of God."

On the other hand, it is equally unfair to the Bible to accuse it of error because it uses the common words and expressions of the ancient Near East. Must we hold that because the Scriptures use expressions like the "third heaven" as equivalent to "Paradise" (the dwelling place of God), the Bible therefore *teaches* a "three-decker" universe? The charge is simply unfair, just as unfair as trying to find references in Scripture to the sphericity of the earth or the movement of the earth in its orbit around the sun. The Bible was not given to teach *any* kind of science. And the fact that it uses the only terminology available—like *firmament* in Genesis 1—cannot fairly be adduced as evidence of erroneous teaching. It is unsound to attach to words all the overtones of meaning which they may at one time have had associated with them. For example, it would appear that the contemporary word *commencement* should have the meaning, "beginning." But when used in academic circles now it commonly refers to the *termination* ceremony of an academic course. The word *lunatic* may have originated in a day when emotional illness was in the minds of men tied to the moon *(luna)*. But those associations have long since been lost. It is highly questionable to try to pin onto various Hebrew words all the unscientific associations to which a study of the cognate languages may point. Let us use the Bible honestly, getting from it the *message* which God intends us to get. Let us not abuse it, either by looking for modern science, or by attributing to it prescientific errors. It is simply *not* the intention of Scripture to present either of these two types of information, true science or erroneous "science." It *is* its purpose to "make . . . [us] wise unto salvation through faith which is in Christ Jesus. [For] all scripture is given by God, and is profitable for doctrine [for teaching Christian truth] , for reproof [of sin] , for correction [of error] , for instruction in righteousness: that the man of God may be perfect [mature] , throughly furnished [equipped] unto all good works" (II Timothy 3:15-17). And this is precisely the role which the Bible plays when Christians read it, meditate upon it, believe it, and obey it!

Literary Criticism

Evangelical believers are sometimes also troubled by the conclusions of the higher critics on such matters as the documentary hypothesis of the Hexateuch, the theory which cuts up the first six books of the Bible into various strands of tradition which were gradually put together, so it is said, during the later centuries of Israel's national life. Two generations ago it was often asserted that there were as many as a dozen strands which could be isolated in the Hexateuch. In reference to this theory, several observations may be made: (1) The critics are growing more cautious and sober, and some scholars have now reduced the number of supposed documents to only three or four, the common ones being listed as J (in which the Lord was called *Jahweh*), E (in which He was called *Elohim*), D (the Book of Deuteronomy), and P (the Priestly code). (2) In the second place, whatever historical process God may have permitted in the writing of the Hexateuch, the full truthfulness and trustworthiness of the Scripture still stands, for our Lord and His apostles accepted the reliability of the Hebrew Scriptures *as written*; and it is Christ's view which is normative for the Christian Church. (3) Finally, it should be observed that the documentary hypothesis may be displaced by a more conservative view. For Biblical critics are steadily growing more cautious and conservative, partly through the impact of more conservative streams of theology, and partly through the findings of archaeology which have vindicated the claims of the Bible on one point after another. In 1924, for example, the learned German scholar, Hugo Gressman, said rather sharply that it must be emphasized "that today there is no science of the Old Testament which does not rest on the foundation of the critical source analysis of the Hexateuch" (*Z.a.t.W.*, 1924, p. 2). But only a decade later, when Professor Umberto Cassuto of the Hebrew University of Jerusalem published his Italian monograph, *La Questione della Genesi* (University of Florence, 1934), the new editor of the *Zeitschrift für die alttestamentliche Wissenschaft* reviewed it with respect, noting that Cassuto held to the objective truth (*Richtigkeit*) of the tradition which is written down in Genesis, calling his monograph a *wertvollen Beitrag* (worthy contribution), and stating that it deserves attention (*Z.a.t.W.*, 1934, pp. 291, 292). Cassuto later embodied his material in a series of brilliant lectures in Hebrew, powerfully refuting on critical grounds the whole documentary hypothesis. Unfortunately, the linguistic barrier long prevented Western scholars from profiting from these lectures. But as early as 1951 H. H. Rowley had remarked that the Graf-Wellhausen view was "only a working hypothesis"; Rowley held that it should be retained until a better view was found, at which point, he said, it could be "abandoned with alacrity" (*The Growth of the O.T.*, p. 46)! Finally, in 1961 the first English edition of Cassuto, *The Documentary Hypothesis*, was published by the Magnes Press, The Hebrew University, Jerusalem, and distributed in the British Commonwealth and Europe by the Oxford University Press. Cassuto's critical analysis of the documentary hypothesis is deserving of careful study. The translator, Israel Abrahams, comments in his Foreword that the result of Professor Cassuto's work is "not so much a scientific edifice laid in ruins as the reaffirmation of the Torah's literary and artistic integrity . . ." (q.v.).

At what point the Pentateuch took its final form we may not be able to answer on critical grounds. We do know that Moses was instructed of God to write at least part of the history of Israel, as well as the law of God. Exodus 17:14; 24:4; 34:27; Numbers 33:2; Deuteronomy 17:18; 31:9, 24-26; 28:58, 61; 29:20-27; 30:10; 31:24. And we soon read of "the book of the law of Moses" (Joshua 8:31, 34; 23:6). For the history prior to his own day Moses may have made use of "whatever oral and written sources" were available. (Harold Lindsell, *Harper Study Bible*, Harper & Row, 1964, p. 1.) We know also that some explanatory notes were inserted into the writings of Moses at a later day. Included in this category is the explanation that the city of Ur was "Ur *of the Chaldees*" [Chaldeans] (Genesis 11:28); the comment in Genesis 12:6 that "*the Canaanite was then in the land*"; a similar note in Genesis 13:7 that "*the Canaanite and the Perizzite dwelled then in the land*"; and the replacement of *Laish* by *Dan* (the later name of the place) in Genesis 14:14. This type of modernizing the text, and adding words to clarify and make more understandable the ancient text of the Pentateuch, is a perfectly natural and legitimate process. (If a new edition of the King James Version were to replace the word *let* in Romans 1:13 by the real meaning, which is *hindered*, we could still call it the King James Version!) Whether these occasional glosses were made informally by later copyists, or more or less officially by such a great figure as "Ezra the Scribe," we cannot now determine.

In any case, notice should here be taken of the Jewish tradition that to Ezra was entrusted the huge task of writing the entire Old Testament from memory! The story is recorded in the Jewish book, IV Ezra (2 Esdras) 14. There we are told of the distress of Ezra over the fact that the holy law of God had been destroyed by fire, and he prayed for divine enablement to write everything which had occurred since the beginning of the world! Sure enough, the Lord heard his petition, and gave him a cup to drink containing a fluid the color of fire. This potion really stimulated him, and for forty days he dictated to five scribes who were divinely enabled to put down the dictation which Ezra gave them in characters which they themselves did not know! Ezra thus wrote not only the twenty-four books of the Hebrew canon—identical with our thirty-nine books—but also seventy other apocryphal books! The legend indicates that when the massive dictation job was accomplished, the Lord authorized Ezra to publish the twenty-four books, but to reserve the seventy others to the wise ones among the Jewish people! (R. H. Charles, *The Apocrypha and Pseudepigrapha of the Old Testament*, II, pp. 620-24.)

Now it is obvious that the legend has gathered a considerable amount of imaginary accretions during the years. And yet it is doubtful if the whole account is pure fiction. It is rather likely that Ezra wrote Chronicles (which is actually the Jewish tradition), and it is entirely probable that he also played a major role under God in the determination of the Hebrew canon—a fact which is considerably exaggerated in the word of IV Ezra that the Lord told Ezra to publish the twenty-four books. It is also to be expected that a man of the stature and significance of Ezra would have done some minor editing of various books of the Old Testament, such as replacing unknown ancient Hebrew words with familiar contemporary Aramaic words. The Jewish rabbis, incidentally, regarded Ezra as a "Second Moses"—and that with good reason.

Christ and the Scriptures

It is indeed true that we are in no position to judge how nearly the older books of the Hebrew canon have come down to us in their exact original form, and how much editing may have been done by later men of God such as Ezra. Of one thing we may be certain, however. *It was the Old Testament, almost exactly as we have it, which our Lord knew, and which He assured us was the infallible truth of God.* And the Dead Sea Scrolls, it may be observed, tend to confirm the substantial accuracy of the Masoretic text of the Old Testament. It should also be mentioned that the writers of the Old Testament historical books have at least to some extent taken us into their confidence by citing about a dozen and a half literary sources: the Book of the Wars of the Lord, the Book of Jashar [or, of the Upright] , the Book of the Chronicles of the Kings of Israel, the Book of the Chronicles of the Kings of Judah, the Books of the Kings of Judah and Israel, the Book of the Acts of Solomon, the Chronicles of Samuel the Seer, the Chronicles of Nathan the Prophet, the History of Nathan the Prophet, the Chronicles of Gad the Seer, the Prophecy of Ahijah the Shilonite, the Visions of Iddo the Seer, the Chronicles of Iddo the Seer, the Chronicles of Shemaiah the Prophet, the Chronicles of Jehu the Son of Hanani, the Commentary on the Book of the Kings, the Vision of Isaiah the Son of Amoz in the Books of the Kings of Judah and Israel, and the Chronicles of the Seers [or, of Hozai]. Numbers 21:14; Joshua 10:13; II Samuel 1:18; I Kings 11: 41; 14:19, 29; I Chronicles 29:29; II Chronicles 9:29; 12:15; 16:11; 24:27; 25:26; 26:22; 28:26; 32:32; 33:19.

How Name Our Doctrine of Inspiration?

If all the Scripture is inspired of God and normative for Christian doctrine, what name should be applied to a sound doctrine of inspiration? It should be said right at the outset in the discussion of this question that the *fact* of inspiration is certain, regardless of what *name* may be applied to it. For Christ, the reliability of Scripture for faith and life extended even to what might be called the fine points of Scripture; He put it vividly: Neither an *iota* (smallest letter) nor a *keraia* (smallest part of a letter) would perish until all is fulfilled. Matthew 5:18. And we have already noted many other assurances from the Lord and His apostles. But what name should be assigned to an adequate theory of inspiration? Two words in particular are advanced by conservative Bible students: *verbal* (meaning that the

reliability of Scripture extends to the very words)—a position which
seems to have appealed to John Baillie *(Idea of Revelation,* p. 115)—
and *plenary* (meaning that all the Scripture is inspired of God). The
word *plenary* is rejected by some scholars because they feel that it
suggests that all the Scripture is equally rich in spiritual content—
which is obviously not the case. The word *verbal* is also not altogeth-
er a happy term for some scholars, for they feel that it suggests that it
was the Holy Spirit who chose the very words which the writers of
Scripture employed—and this too is obviously untrue, for as a matter of fact each Biblical writer has his own vocabulary and style.
Some scholars feel that a new term, *dynamical,* would best express
the paradox that the Scriptures are the very Word of God, yet written in the words of men, but this word has also failed to meet with
widespread acceptance. Perhaps it is wisest not to insist on a human
name for an obvious mystery, but simply to assert with the Scriptures that *the Bible was written by holy men of God who were borne
of the Holy Spirit so effectively that all Scripture is "God-given,"
and therefore normative for faith and life.*

It is indeed fortunate that the authority of Scripture does not
depend upon any human theory of inspiration. As long ago as 1881
two Presbyterian evangelicals, B. B. Warfield and A. A. Hodge,
wrote: "Nor should we ever allow it to be believed that the truth of
Christianity depends upon any doctrine of inspiration whatever.
Revelation came in large part before the record of it, and the Christian Church before the New Testament Scriptures. Inspiration can
have no meaning if Christianity is not true, but Christianity would
be true and divine, and being so, would stand, even if God had not
been pleased to give us, in addition to His revelation of saving truth,
an infallible record of that revelation absolutely errorless by means
of inspiration" *(Presbyterian Review,* Ap. 1881, p. 227). And James
Orr, after citing this, and after discussing various views of inspiration, gets to the essence of the matter when he speaks of "this unde-
niable, self-attesting, spiritual quality of Scripture" *(Revelation and
Inspiration,* 1910, p. 201). And we must once more tie our doctrine
of inspiration, just as our doctrine of Biblical authority, to the purpose of Scripture. And that purpose was not to give us an all-com-

prehensive history of the human race, nor to make such detailed scientific revelations as would make human research unnecessary. Rather, *the purpose* of the Bible is to witness to Christ and His salvation. As Orr put it in 1910: "The Bible has the qualities claimed for it as an inspired book. These qualities . . . nothing but inspiration could impart. It leads to God and to Christ; it gives light on the deepest problems of life, death, and eternity; it discovers [to us] the way of deliverance from sin; it makes men new creatures; it furnishes the man of God completely for every good work. That it possesses these qualities history and experience through all the centuries have attested. . . . The word of God is a 'pure word.' It is a true and 'tried' word; a word never found wanting by those who rest themselves upon it" *(Revelation and Inspiration*, pp. 218, 219).

The Holy Spirit and Scripture

Only one word remains to be said. Just as the Scripture is not an end in itself, but fulfills its God-intended role by leading men to the Saviour of the world, the incarnate Word of God, so likewise we must not look upon the Scriptures apart from the blessed ministry of the Holy Spirit in the hearts of those who read that inscripturated Word. The Scripture itself witnesses to this important and essential truth. "The natural man," writes Paul of the man who is devoid of the Spirit of God, "receiveth not the things of the Spirit of God: for they are foolishness unto him: neither can he know them, because they are spiritually discerned" (I Corinthians 2:14). This blindness to spiritual reality on the part of the unregenerated man stands in contrast with us believers who have received "the spirit which is of God; that we might know the things that are freely given to us of God" (I Corinthians 2:12). We are Christ's epistle, for "the Spirit of the living God" has inscribed His "writing" in the fleshy [tablets] of the heart" (II Corinthians 3:3). Paul lamented that in his day a veil of unbelief rested over the hearts of many of his Jewish brethren, effectively blinding them to the Bible's true witness: that is, its witness to Christ: "Until this day remaineth the same vail untaken away in the reading of the old testament; which vail is done away in Christ. But even unto this day, when Moses is read, the vail is upon their heart'' (II Corinthians 3:14, 15). Paul looked to the day when the Holy Spirit would bring these blind Bible readers to saving faith in Christ, for then, and only then, shall the veil be taken away. II Corinthians 3:16. To those of us who have been graciously brought to saving faith in Christ by the blessed Holy Spirit Paul writes: ''But we all, with open [unveiled] face beholding as in a glass the glory of the Lord, are [being] changed into the same image from glory to glory even as by the Spirit of the Lord'' (II Corinthians 3:18). In the final analysis, therefore, the authority of the Bible is perceived only by those who are in Christ and who are therefore indwelt by His Holy Spirit.

Veni, Spiritus Creator,
mentes tuorum visita!
Creator Spirit, Do Thou alone
Come into the Minds which are Thine own!

3
THE MEANING OF SCRIPTURE

Need to Interpret

At the very outset of this discussion, there will perhaps be those who question its necessity. Do we not believe, they ask, that the Scriptures possess genuine clarity? Did not Jeremiah look down the vistas of the centuries to the era of the new covenant and describe that era as one in which the saints of God will have no need of mutual teaching? Jeremiah 31:34. And do not the apostles Paul and John both indicate that this is precisely the situation in which Christian believers now find themselves? I Thessalonians 4:9; I John 2:20-27. About all that can be said at this point is that this sufficiency of the individual believer is a relative matter, that it is only in respect to the most basic essentials of Christianity that the Holy Spirit makes mutual Christian teaching unnecessary. The need for the study of the meaning of Scripture arises from inequalities which we must confess do exist among the saints of Christ. Who can deny that believers differ as to the extent of their knowledge? It is also evident that God has endowed some of His children with massive intellectual and spiritual power which enables them to grasp with unusual insight and comprehensiveness the basic truths of Christianity, and their wide implications for human thought. Such examples as the Apostle Paul, Augustine, Luther, Calvin, B. B. Warfield, Karl Barth, and Emil Brunner are evidence of the influential role which certain of God's servants of the Word have played in the history of the church. And although it is true that there is a fundamental sense in which the individual Christian stands on his own feet as he reads God's Word, yet it must be pointed out that the New Testament also explicitly recognizes the value of brotherly instruction. I Corinthians 3: 2; II Timothy 2:2; Galatians 2:11; Hebrews 5:11, 12. Indeed, the very writing of the New Testament books and letters was in itself basic evidence of the value of brotherly admonition and instruction.

The Reformers

We will need to pass over here that which is well covered by many works on the history of interpretation, namely, the story of Jewish hermeneutics, and ancient, medieval, Reformation, and modern schools of interpreters. Suffice it to say that the historic allegorical method of interpretation, regardless of how "spiritual" it may have seemed, and how "respectable" it may have made the Word of God appear to the generations of the ages past, justly met its end in the reformers of the sixteenth century. God used men like Luther, Zwingli, and Calvin to do away with the "monkey business" of allegorization (as Luther called it), and to lead the church once more to a better hermeneutic. One is tempted to say, To lead the church once more to the genuine meaning of the Scriptures, for that is precisely how the reformers regarded their hermeneutics—and with considerable justification.

It will not be possible in our brief treatment to analyze the unique strengths and weaknesses of the major works on interpretation of the last hundred years. (Note especially the monographs of Frederic W. Farrar, Robert M. Grant, and James D. Wood.) Special mention must also be made of the treatises by J. C. K. von Hofmann, *Interpreting the Bible* (original lectures, 1860; published in German, 1880, first English edition, 1959); Milton S. Terry, *Biblical Hermeneutics* (first edition, 1883; last reprint, 1961); Bernard Ramm, *Protestant Biblical Interpretation* (revised edition, 1956); James D. Smart, *The Interpretation of Scripture* (1961); *The New Hermeneutic,* edited by James M. Robinson and John B. Cobb, Jr. (1964); and especially of the fine work of A. Berkeley Mickelsen, *Interpreting the Bible* (1963). In my own thinking, however, I have been most influenced by the essays of Louis Berkhof, *Principles of Biblical Interpre-*

tation (1950), as the following discussion will indicate.

What then was the great contribution of the reformers? Put in a positive way, it was the central emphasis of the reformers to take what might be called the "plain sense" of the Scriptures, basing every exegetical conclusion upon the meaning of the original language, and interpreting the figurative language of the Bible by those passages in which literal language is found. The reformers had a strong sense of the historical, of God's saving acts, particularly of His saving acts in Christ: the incarnation, death, and resurrection of the Lord Jesus, and the fullness of the revelation of God in His personal and incarnate Word. It is no accident that the study of both Hebrew and Greek largely came to its own among the Protestants of the sixteenth century. (However, Reuchlin, a Catholic, took the lead in Hebrew, and Erasmus in Greek.) The reformers held to the doctrine that the Bible has but one true sense in each passage. They rejected the medieval three- or fourfold sense of Scripture (literal, tropological, allegorical, and anagogical). Luther stressed what has been called the right of private interpretation, a doctrine which certainly does not mean that every Tom, Dick, and Harry can set up his private interpretation against the sound and trustworthy interpretative tradition of the church of Christ—although some Protestants give one the impression that this is what they believe—but rather in the sense that there is only one true meaning in any given statement in God's Word, and it is the Holy Spirit who enables His saints to attain that meaning. In other words, *the church must ever stand ready to correct its traditional interpretation by the written Word.* Luther saw a great need for just such correction in his day, and he proceeded with great energy and courage to offer the needed correction of the tradition. Luther saw also the importance of personal faith on the part of him who was hearing or reading God's Word, if he was rightly to understand it. Luther's greatest contribution as a scholar was certainly his German Bible translation, first the New Testament (1522) and later the entire Bible (1534). Luther did believe, of course, that common people could read the Word of God in their own tongue, and to their immense spiritual profit—not in the sense that they could understand it better than the exegetical princes of the church, but in the sense that the people were entitled to the Word of God both in its preached form and in its inscripturated form.

For Luther the Scriptures were person-centered. The chief function of the inscripturated Word was to witness to the Incarnate Word, the Lord Jesus, and to the great doctrine of justification by faith—the doctrine which Luther had in his own experience discovered through a most difficult struggle, with much agony of soul. This doctrine of justification by faith was for Luther the very touchstone of apostolicity in the writings which the church offered to the faithful as canonical. Luther was also aware how significant the context of any given passage was—and here he was not breaking new ground, for scholars as early as John Wyclif had written (cited by Wilbur M. Smith, *Profitable Bible Study*, Wilde, 1939, p. 38):

> It shall greatly helpe ye
> > to understande Scripture,
> If thou mark
> Not only what is spoken or wrytten,
> But of whom,
> And to whom,
> With what words,
> At what time,
> Where,
> To what intent,
> With what circumstances,
> Considering what goeth before
> And what followeth.

Had Luther written this, he would have undoubtedly emphasized also the Christ-witness of the Scriptures, because for him the value of the Scriptures was that they were the crib which held the Lord Jesus. Luther stressed also the necessity of the church coming under the authority of the Word. Neither pope nor council dared, asserted Luther, to say or teach anything contrary to the content of the Holy Scriptures. His emphasis on the Christ-witness of the Bible; on the central truth of the Gospel, justification by faith; and his extremely successful effort to make the Bible writers "speak

Deutsch": these are the major contributions of the doctor of Wittenberg to the renewal of the church of Christ in the sixteenth century.

If Luther is the initial reformer and the great Bible translator, Calvin is easily the theologian of the Reformation, and the Biblical exegete. Seldom indeed has the church been blessed with a man who could so surely place his finger on the meaning of Holy Scripture as could Calvin. He too had a Christocentric Bible in the best sense of the phrase, but he was too careful an exegete to call every psalm Messianic just because Christ is referred to in some psalms. Calvin's commentaries may still be consulted with immense profit.

The Anabaptists

The evangelical and non-revolutionary Anabaptists of Switzerland, Austria, Germany, and the Netherlands, were somewhat of a trial to the leading reformers because of their radical views on the nature of the church and of the Christian ethic. These Anabaptists felt that Luther and Zwingli had stopped short of going all the way with the Scriptures in correcting the tradition of the church. It was fine, said the Anabaptists, that required fasts, compulsory clerical celibacy, the mass, the papacy, the concept of meritorious good works, and other accretions of church history which violated Scriptural principles, had been rejected and abolished by the reformers. But why, asked the Anabaptist leaders—such as Conrad Grebel and Felix Manz in Switzerland, Michael Sattler and Pilgram Marpeck in Germany, and Obbe and Dirk Philips in the Netherlands—do the great reformers not go all the way with the Scriptures and abolish the state and people's church, infant baptism, and any office or activity which violates New Testament *agape* love? (For the Anabaptists this meant withdrawing from both the military and the magistracy—both of which institutions involved the imposition of the death penalty.) These issues involved a major problem in the interpretation of the Bible. What really is the relation of the Old Testament to the New? To what portions, if any, of the Old Testament may the church appeal? The reformers took the position that the ceremonial laws of the Old Testament were done away, such as clean and unclean foods, animal sacrifices, the institution of the priesthood, and the like. The Anabaptists agreed, but also thought that Christians should not justify compulsion in matters of faith by an appeal to the Old Testament, nor infant baptism, nor participation in warfare. The old covenant, they insisted, has been replaced by its perfect fulfillment (Hebrews 8:6, 7), the New Testament. It is therefore an unwarranted and impossible procedure for the church to cast aside clear New Testament directives in order to return to the preparatory Old Testament to find justification for such non-Christian institutions and practices as the state church, infant baptism, participation in warfare, and the use of force and bloodshed in matters of conscience.

Sola Scriptura

The Reformation of the sixteenth century broke Western Christendom into Roman Catholic, Lutheran, Reformed, Anabaptist, and Anglican camps—all appealing to the Scriptures as their final court of appeal, except that the Catholics never did accept the Protestant principle of *sola scriptura* (sole authority of the Scriptures). It may be mentioned in passing that various Protestant scholars now feel that Protestant strictures may have been drawn a bit too severely against tradition in the sixteenth century, for in very truth there actually is an ongoing "tradition" of interpretation and practice in the Christian Church which gives it basic stability and vital continuity from age to age—provided such tradition remains subject to continual correction and scrutiny from God's inscripturated Word. At the same time, there are now also faint beginnings which may lead ultimately to the demotion of Tradition from its present place as an equal partner with Scripture in the determination of the doctrine and practice of the Roman Church. The Jesuit theologian, Karl Rahner, has declared in print that the Catholic Church may need to surrender its "Two Sources Theory" of authority, Scripture and Tradition, and return to the position which recognizes the ultimacy of Biblical authority in the life of Christ's church. (*Inspiration in the Bible* [a poor translation of the German original title, *Über die Schrift-inspiration*], fourth impression, 1963, pp. 30-38.)

Helps

What are the tools which will aid the interpreter of the Bible to arrive at sound doctrinal conclusions? It need hardly be said that it is obviously only the Bible in the original tongues which can be taken as the foundational text of God's Word written. No translation is ever quite perfect. The first-rate Bible interpreter will seek therefore to learn to read the Scriptures for himself in both Hebrew and Aramaic, and in *Koine* Greek. He will of course also make use of the best grammars, lexicons, concordances, and commentaries based on the text of the original languages. He will secure the most reliable books in Biblical introduction, Biblical history, and Biblical theology for both the Old and New Testaments. He will get all the light he can from authors who have studied the history of interpretation. And he will read from a wide spectrum of commentators, men from various Christian communions, to quicken his awareness of varying ways of understanding God's Word. He will also be a holy man of God, born again, sanctified, and filled with the Spirit, and a man of much prayer: for the spiritual qualities are even more important in the interpreter than the academic tools.

But what if a given Christian has never had opportunity to attain sufficient facility in the languages of Scripture to form sound judgments based on the study of the Greek and Hebrew texts? How then may one become as good an interpreter as possible? The use of a wide variety of good versions is a genuine help in arriving at the meaning of a given statement in Scripture. (The accuracy with which a given version has been made may be given a crude test by checking on two pairs of widely separated verses which read verbatim in the original: Isaiah 35:10 and 51:11; and Matthew 26:41 and Mark 14:38.)

Grammatical Interpretation

Let us now attempt to formulate the major guides which good Bible interpreters have found useful. The first rule is this: *Seek to determine as carefully as possible the exact meaning of the text, using the best scholarly helps, studying the context, examining parallel or similar statements, and asking honestly: What does the language mean?* Sometimes the meaning of a given statement will hang in a major way on a key word—such as "cross," or "Spirit," or "flesh." Word studies may then be helpful. But at this point the Bible student also needs to remember that we do not overemphasize etymology—for that process can be as misleading as allegorization. Ignorant people are impressed with the wealth of information which "deep scholarship" can draw from a single word—when as a matter of simple fact, the word when used by the writer did not any longer bear many of the meanings which its history suggests. The meaning of words is ever a matter of contemporary usage, not of etymology. And the rule works two ways. For the words of the Greek New Testament have often had a wealth of meaning *added* to them through the life and death of Jesus Christ. Hence words like "Christ," "cross," "salvation," "grace," and "life" have a far richer meaning in the New Testament than they did in non-Christian and in pre-Christian Greek circles. Furthermore, we do not study one word after another, and then pile up their meanings like bricks. On the contrary we study the syntax carefully. What is the force of this articular infinitive? Is this participle temporal or causative? Is the mood of this verb indicative or imperative?

The most difficult questions arise in connection with figures of speech, and the Bible abounds with all kinds of figures. A *metaphor* calls an object by the term which it resembles. If Herod Antipas was a sly thief, capable of stealing his own brother's wife, Jesus by a metaphor could call him a "fox" (Luke 13:32). If Christians are dependent upon Christ for their spiritual life, Christ is the "vine," and believers are the "branches" (John 15:5). *Metonymy* calls one thing another because of a mental association. To have "Moses and the prophets" means, of course, to have their writings. Luke 16:29. *Synecdoche* is a similar figure, used when there actually is a close connection between two things: for example, the cup and its contents: "This cup is the new testament in my blood," means, of course, The contents of this cup are a memorial of my blood. A *parable* is a perfectly natural story ("Behold, a sower went forth to sow"), while an *allegory* is an artificial story such as the account of the trees talking and choosing a king. Judges 9:8. Mention must be made of *obvious exaggeration* for the sake of emphasis: Never invite anyone into your house who might in turn invite you into his (Luke 14:12)—the point being, Forget about your social "level," be genuinely hospitable, and show compassion to the poor! A *euphemism* is the use of a mild term to express gently or with good taste something more serious. Instead of saying that a man died, the Bible may say that he "fell asleep" (Acts 7:60). *Zeugma* is the yoking of two ideas, while fully expressing only one: such as the exhortation in Hebrews 12:12. The writer wishes his readers to "lift" their hands in glad activity, and to straighten up the sagging knees—but he does not bother to write the second verb: "Lift up the hands which hang down, and . . . the feeble knees." The reader's mind is of course supposed to supply a suitable verb, such as strengthen, or straighten up. (Any thorough study of Bible interpretation will have a complete list of Biblical figures.)

The real problem in the area of figurative language is not figures of speech, for generally a figure is obviously such. The real problem is language which is understandable literally, and which may nevertheless have a deeper spiritual meaning than the words indicate. Isaiah prophesies,

> The desert shall rejoice,
> and blossom as the rose,

Is this prophecy an indication of future fruitfulness for the desert? Or is it perhaps a prophecy of the joy which the children of God shall have when God acts redemptively in their behalf? The prophet goes on,

> It shall blossom abundantly,
> and rejoice
> even with joy and singing (Isaiah 35:1, 2).

Since deserts cannot literally sing, we are compelled to ask whether the whole section may not be figurative rather than literal. (Let no one say that this is emptying the Bible of meaning, for the joys of God's redemption in the hearts of His children are infinitely more significant than making flowers grow in sandy soil.) The context in statements such as the above is often helpful in discerning the meaning.

> The mountains and the hills shall break forth
>> before you into singing,
> and all the trees of the field
>> shall clap their hands.
> Instead of the thorn
>> shall come up the fir tree.
> and instead of the brier
>> shall come up the myrtle tree . . . (Isaiah 55:12, 13).

As indicated earlier, special emphasis must be placed upon the crucial importance of *context* in the interpretation of every sentence in the Bible. Is the context one of narrative, or of prophetic or apostolic teaching? Is the statement that of a spokesman for God, or merely the account of what some wicked person said or did? If the Lord condemned the doctrines of Eliphaz, Bildad, and Zophar, would it be a sound procedure to quote their comments as authoritative Scripture? Context therefore means the immediate situation in which a given verse stands; it means also the entire book in which it is found, and ultimately the whole corpus of divine revelation. And this brings us to a most important truth. *The best interpreter of the Bible is the Bible itself.* The child of God who reads through the Bible time after time with close attention will find one passage after another, which was formerly locked shut to his understanding, opening up and becoming perspicuous.

Historical Interpretation

This brings us to our second major principle of interpretation. *Gather as much information on the historical background of the Scriptures as possible.* In a general way, the original readers were in a favorable position to understand the allusions of each writer, the sins against which he warns, the duties he feels impelled to emphasize, and so on. Americans today understand fully when they hear a busy person complain that he has "a hundred and one things" to do. It does not mean one more than a hundred; in fact, it might mean five urgent matters demanding attention and action at the same time. Or if one speaks of the communist threat, saying, "Somehow Moscow has me worried," the meaning of Moscow is clear: it refers to the governmental policy of the Union of Soviet Socialist Republics. In the Biblical world there were also figures of speech, and allusions to contemporary threats. Isaiah 46:11 speaks of "a ravenous bird from the east"—surely an example of an unclear allusion for an American reader of two and a half millennia later! The prophet helps us a bit by adding a parallel line, "the man that executeth my counsel from a far country." A careful study of the context of this prophecy seems to indicate that God is going to raise up a military figure who will deliver Judah from her Babylonian captivity, a man who will evidently restore Israel to her homeland, exchanging Babylon for Jerusalem. (Compare Isaiah 46:13; 44:28, and 45:13.) In the Old Testament there are continual references to Egypt, Syria, Assyria, Edom, Babylonia, and other nations and peoples. The more one knows of the life and history of these nations and peoples, the clearer will be the Biblical references to them. In the Revelation, for example, one reads of "Gog and Magog," a phrase which has no meaning to the common reader today. But if one consults a good Bible dictionary, he will find that Gog and Magog refer to a wicked prince and a heathen people from the north of Israel, perhaps from Southern Russia. To the Jews in the time of Ezekiel—and the language is reflecting Ezekiel in the Revelation of John (Revelation 20:8)—Gog and Magog were symbolic of a heathen threat to God's people, a threat which was formidable indeed. The "hornet" of Exodus 23:28 and Joshua 24:12 may refer to Egypt—for the bee was the symbol of Egypt in the hieroglyphics.

These illustrations help us realize that the more we know of the history, life, government, religious views, and practices, both of Israel and of the surrounding nations, the better the position we are in to understand the Bible. Archaeology is a great help to Bible scholars, for it reveals much of the way of life, the weights, measures, and money of the lands being investigated. I Samuel 13:19-22, for example, is a historical account of the period in Israel's history when the nation was too weak to stand up against the Philistines, a warlike people which had migrated to Canaan in ancient times, perhaps from the island of Crete. (Indeed the name Palestine is a corruption of Philistine [land].) The strong Philistines in the days of Saul were able to forbid the Israelites to work in iron, thus keeping them from manufacturing swords and spears of war. Consequently, the Israelites had to go to the Philistine smiths to have their tools sharpened. There is a Hebrew word used in I Samuel 13:21, spelled PIM, which was a total puzzle to the English Bible translators until modern times. The translators simply did not know what a *pim* was. Could the word perhaps mean a file? The translators had to write something; so tongue in cheek they wrote, "yet they had a file. . . ." The American Standard Version of 1901 added the honest marginal note: "The Hebrew text is obscure." At this point archaeology now comes to our assistance. Seven weights, marked PIM, have been found in Palestine, ranging in weight from 7.18 to 8.13 grams, which is roughly two-thirds of a shekel, or one fourth of an ounce. The RSV revisers were therefore able to clear up the obscurity: "The charge was a *pim*"—which may have been rather exorbitant, as John B. Graybill suggests. (*Zondervan Pictorial Bible Dictionary*, p. 892.) Incidentally, the Septuagint translators seem to have gotten closer to the meaning than did the translators of the English Bible. And this is of great interest to us. The ancient versions of the Bible, such as the Greek Old Testament, the so-called Septuagint, sometimes throw real light on the Old Testament, particularly where there seems to be some textual corruption. Hence English Bibles frequently have marginal notes indicating how the ancient versions read.

Works such as Bible dictionaries and encyclopedias throw much light on the meaning of Bible verses by identifying for us various plants, animals, birds, coins, weights, and measures of the Biblical world. The older English Bibles sometimes had poor translations of certain Hebrew words. "Unicorn" is an example. The average reader thinks of a mythical creature having a single horn projecting from its head. What is the animal which the older English versions designated as the "unicorn"? It was a huge wild ox known as the *Aurochs*—and when seen in profile appeared to have but one horn! Modern English versions read, *wild ox*. A similar improvement has been made in the translation of a Hebrew word which is translated in the King James Version as "groves." The Hebrew word seems to refer to wooden pillars or images of the female deity *Asherah*, perhaps a

Phoenician goddess originally, but also corresponding to the Babylonia *Ishtar*, the goddess of human love and fertility. This goddess *Asherah* is associated in the Old Testament with *Baal*, the fertility god of the Canaanites. Lascivious and abominable rites were associated with this idolatry. Were one to read only of the "groves" in the older English versions, without consulting Bible dictionaries or encyclopedias, one would not understand the term at all. *Historical interpretation means getting a proper understanding of the Bible by securing all the assistance which historical research is able to provide.*

Relation of the Two Testaments

Paradoxically, we must hold both to the *unity* and to the *diversity* of the Bible, for each Biblical book has its own unique characteristics and emphases. The greatest difference is between the books of the Old Testament, which of course were written prior to the incarnation and passion of our Lord, and the books of the New Testament, which were written after Pentecost and the establishment of the Christian Church. And yet there is a basic unity, both within the books of each Testament, and as between the two Testaments as well. We find the same spiritual needs of men recognized in both Testaments, and the same seeking and redemptive God at work in the redemption of men and the creation of a people for His name. Jeremiah anticipated that there would be a new covenant with superior spiritual blessings. In beautiful poetry he wrote,

> Behold, the days come, saith the Lord,
> > that I will make a new covenant
> > with the house of Israel,
> > and with the house of Judah:
> > not according to the covenant that I made
> > with their fathers
> > in the day
> > that I took them by the hand
> > to bring them out of the land of Egypt;
> > which my covenant they brake,
> > although I was an husband unto them,

> saith the Lord:
> But this shall be the covenant that I will make
>> with the house of Israel;
>> After those days,
>> saith the Lord,
> I will put my law in their inward parts,
>> and write it in their hearts;
>> and will be their God,
>> and they shall be my people.
> And they shall teach no more
>> every man his neighbour,
>> and every man his brother, saying,
>> Know the Lord:
> for they shall all know me,
>> from the least of them
>> unto the greatest of them,
>> saith the Lord:
> for I will forgive their iniquity,
>> and I will remember their sins
>> no more (Jeremiah 31:31-34).

This is the new covenant with Israel, including the "Israel" of faith, not just those racially of Israel, which the Lord Jesus made with His own precious blood: "This is," solemnly declared Jesus the night of His betrayal, "my blood of the new testament [covenant], which is shed for many" (Mark 14:24). And the writer of Hebrews declared that Christ has "obtained a more excellent ministry [than Moses], by how much also he is the mediator of a better covenant, which was established upon better promises. For if that first covenant had been faultless, then should no place have been sought for the second" (Hebrews 8:6, 7). The writer then goes on to quote Jeremiah 31 in support of the divine promise to establish this new covenant.

It was the Anabaptists of the sixteenth century who emphasized the superiority of the new covenant and its implications for Christian theology and Christian ethics. One of the most reliable interpreters of Anabaptism wrote:

"Regarding the relation of the Old Testament Scriptures to the New Testament the Brethren [the Anabaptists] differed fundamentally from state church Protestantism. They believed indeed that all Scripture was given by inspiration of God and is inerrantly true in all its statements and doctrinal teachings. Nevertheless they recognized the fact that the relation of the Old to the New Testament Scriptures is that of promise to fulfillment, of type and shadow to reality, of the groundwork of a building to the building itself. God's promise under the old covenant was that a new covenant was to be established at the coming of the Redeemer; and the New Testament Scriptures teach that Christ is the 'Mediator of a better covenant.'

"A 'faultless covenant' was impossible before Christ's coming and His work of redemption. The Old Testament Scriptures were the rule of life for pre-Messianic times. The New Testament obligations ('The law of Christ,' Galatians 6:2) are more far-reaching and perfect than the Mosaic law. Whatever of the old law is obligatory for the Christian is repeated and taught in the New Testament Scriptures.

"This was the position of the Swiss Brethren and Mennonites concerning the Old Testament. The theologians of the state churches, on the contrary, found themselves compelled to go back to the Old Testament for maintaining the points on which they differed from the Brethren. They believed that in the Old Testament Scriptures they had found ground for defending infant baptism, the union of church and state, the persecution of dissenters, and war, for the followers of Christ. They failed to make the distinction between the Old and New Testament Scriptures on which the Mennonites insisted" (John Horsch, *Mennonites in Europe*, 1950, p. 354). Confirmation of the reliability of the Horsch interpretation has appeared recently with the publication of the monograph of Leonard Verduin, *The Reformers and Their Stepchildren* (Grand Rapids: Eerdmans, 1964). See also the articles "Bible" and "Old Testament" in the *Mennonite Encyclopedia* (Scottdale, Pennsylvania: Mennonite Publishing House, 4 volumes, 1955-59).

It must not be thought that the Old Testament Scriptures are not the Word of God, however. For all Scripture is God-given and therefore profitable. II Timothy 3:16. *The Mennonite Confession of Faith*, adopted by Mennonite General Conference in 1963, states the following on revelation and inspiration (Article 2):

"We believe that the God of creation and redemption has revealed Himself and His will for men in the Holy Scriptures, and supremely and finally in His incarnate Son, the Lord Jesus Christ. God's purpose in this revelation is the salvation of all men. Although God's power and deity are revealed in His creation, so that the nations are without excuse, this knowledge of Him cannot save men, for it cannot make Christ known. God revealed Himself in saving word and deed to Israel as recorded in the Old Testament; He fulfilled this revelation of Himself in the word and deed of Christ as recorded in the New Testament. We believe that all Scripture is given by the inspiration of God, that men moved by the Holy Spirit spoke from God. We accept the Scriptures as the authoritative Word of God, and through the Holy Spirit as the infallible Guide to lead men to faith in Christ and to guide them in the life of Christian discipleship.

"We believe that the Old Testament and the New Testament together constitute the Word of God, that the Old Testament was preparatory, that its institutions were temporary in character, and that the new covenant in Christ is the fulfillment of the old. We believe that the Old Testament writings are inspired and profitable, and as the divine word of promise are to be interpreted in conjunction with the divine act of fulfillment recorded in the New.

"The message of the Bible points to the Lord Jesus Christ. It is to Him that the Scriptures of the Old Testament bear witness, and He is the One whom the Scriptures of the New Testament proclaim. He is the key to the proper understanding of the entire Bible."

Again it must be emphasized that there is a unity to the whole Bible. Both Testaments teach the personality, love, and holiness of God; the sin and need of human beings; the necessity of mediated access to God; His demand for holiness of heart and life in us; our need for meditation and prayer; the creation of all things by God, and His providence in history and life; His grace toward those of faith; the need of divine enablement to live a life pleasing to God;

and life in the hereafter.

Since all Scripture is God-given, there is a God-given unity to the Book. This means that the less clear portions must be interpreted in the light of the more lucid parts. And the Christian scholar who encounters a problem for which he can at the moment find no satisfactory solution must be content to put the problem on the "waiting-shelf" for the time being. On one point there is full clarity in the Scriptures. There is a continuity to the redemptive program of God under the old covenant and in the new. The new birth is a spiritual fulfillment of the sign of the Abrahamic covenant, circumcision. Colossians 2:11, 12. Christ is a spiritual fulfillment of the Passover lamb of the Exodus. I Corinthians 5:7. Just as the blood of the Old Testament sacrifices was spilled, so the Lord Jesus shed His precious blood for our redemption. Hebrews 9:12. The Old Testament had various ceremonial washings and purifications, and similarly we have had our hearts purified by the washing of regeneration and renewal of the Holy Spirit (Titus 3:5); our hearts were sprinkled, and our bodies washed. Hebrews 10:22. Although not all Israelites were saved—there was actually only a believing remnant—yet that believing remnant by entering the church of Christ established a continuity between God's chosen Israel of old, and the new "Israel of God" (Galatians 6:16); the middle wall of partition between Jew and Gentile has been broken down in Christ, and in Him there is one new man, one united body, the church of Christ. Through this continuity, with the Israel of God, the members of the church of Christ are spiritually "Abraham's seed, and heirs" of the promises made to him and his seed. Galatians 3:29. The unity of the Old and New Testaments is a unity in redemption: first fully realized in Christ, however. Hebrews 9:8-15; 10:1-18.

Christological Interpretation

The New Testament also plays a normative role in the interpretation of Messianic prophecy. Our Lord and His apostles furnish us with "sample understandings" of Old Testament predictions of Christ and the church. As the Norwegian theologian, Olav Valen-Sendstad, wrote: If Jesus Christ appeared in human history as the

God-Man, "then He and He alone" has perfect knowledge "in respect to the Scriptures." A Christian theology of the Scriptures will therefore hold to no other view than that which Scripture presents. (Cited by Robert D. Preus in *Christian Faith and Modern Theology*. New York: Channel Press, 1964, p. 114.) We have already seen that Christ drew upon the writings of Moses, those of the prophets, and from Division III of the Hebrew canon, "the Psalms," for His exposition of Messianic prophecy. He Himself stated emphatically, "Do not think that I will accuse you to the Father: there is one that accuseth you, even Moses, in whom ye trust. For had ye believed Moses, ye would have believed me: for he wrote of me. But if ye believe not his writings, how shall ye believe my words" (John 5:45-47)? Philip was in perfect agreement therefore with his Lord when he told Nathanael, "We have found him, of whom Moses in the law, and the prophets, did write, Jesus of Nazareth, the son of Joseph" (John 1: 45). The whole sweep of the Messiah's life was toward the cross; it was His predetermined end, for it was the will of the Father that through His crucified Son the race should be redeemed from the guilt and power of sin. When Jesus began to teach His disciples the necessity of His coming death at Jerusalem, and Peter objected, Jesus rebuked Peter sharply for not aligning his thinking with the will of God. Matthew 16:21-23. "All things which . . . [were] written" had to be fulfilled. Luke 21:22. The early disciples, prior to Pentecost, were actually blind to the necessity of Christ's passion and death. Luke 24:25-27. Jesus declared to His desperate apostles that it would have been in His power to save Himself by "more than twelve legions of angels. But how then . . . [should] the scriptures be fulfilled, that thus it must be" (Matthew 26:53, 54)?

From a spiritual point of view, all history converged on the incarnation, death, and resurrection of the Messiah. The Gospel *kerygma* begins therefore with the startling declaration of Christ Himself: "The time is fulfilled, and the kingdom of God is at hand . . . " (Mark 1:15). And all through His ministry, the phrase keeps occurring that this or that was done, "that the scripture might be fulfilled." The preaching of repentance by John the Baptist was the fulfillment of the Messianic prophecy. Luke carefully dates the be-

ginning of John's significant ministry as the fifteenth year of the
emperor Tiberias [he reigned A.D. 14-37], when Pontius Pilate
was governor [procurator] of Judea [he served A.D. 26-36],
and Annas and Caiaphas were the Jewish high priests. The word of
God came to John, as it had to the great prophets of the Old Testament, "And he came into all the country about Jordan, preaching
the baptism of repentance for the remission of sins; as it is written in
the book of the words of Esaias the prophet [40:3-5], saying,

> The voice of one crying in the wilderness,
>> Prepare ye the way of the Lord,
>> make his paths straight.
> Every valley shall be filled,
> and every mountain and hill
>> shall be brought low;
>> and the crooked shall be made straight,
>> and the rough ways shall be made smooth;
>> and all flesh shall see the salvation of God (Luke 3:1-6).

This use of Isaiah's Messianic proclamation is typical of the way
Christ fulfilled Old Testament prophecy. He fulfilled the passages
which had to do with His natural life (birth at Bethlehem, for example) in a literal sense. And He fulfilled also in their true sense those
Old Testament poetical prophecies which were clothed in figurative
language. He never carried a lamp, but in a spiritual sense, he came
"to give light to them that . . . [sat] in darkness" (Luke 1:79).
Matthew quoted Isaiah (9:2):

> The people which sat in darkness
>> saw great light;
> and to them which sat in the region and shadow
>> of death
>> light is sprung up (Matthew 4:16)

The godly Simeon cried prophetically:

> A light to lighten the Gentiles,
> and the glory of thy people Israel (Luke 2:32).

The New Testament indicates that Jesus perfectly fulfilled the
Messianic intent of the Old Testament Scriptures. The apostles saw
the essential witness of the Old Testament as a witness to the Lord

Jesus and His Messiahship. This theme runs right through the New Testament, *making Christ the unifying bond between the two Testaments: promised in the Old, fulfilled by Jesus in the New*. When Philip found the Ethiopian official reading Isaiah 53, he "began at the same scripture, and preached unto him Jesus" (Acts 8:35). Paul regularly went to the Jewish synagogue on his evangelistic campaigns, and when the opportunity to speak was extended to him, he demonstrated from the Old Testament Scriptures that the Messiah needed to suffer, and that Jesus was the Messiah ("Christ"): Acts 9: 22; 17:3; 18:5, 28; 26:22, 23. The Apostle Peter preached the same message: "Those things, which God before had shewed by the mouth of all his prophets, that [his] Christ should suffer, he hath so fulfilled" (Acts 3:18). Whatever the Old Testament predicted, that the apostles saw fulfilled in Jesus; and whatever Jesus did, that they regarded as having been predicted of the Christ. Everything came to pass just as it had been prophesied.

Christ is therefore the center of the Bible, not only in the sense that the Old Testament prophets witnessed to His coming, and that the New Testament apostles interpreted the significance of His life, teaching, death, and resurrection, but also in the sense that He, and He alone, is the absolute norm of Christian truth and the only full revelation of God. Only He is "the way, and the truth, and the life" (John 14:6). Only He is "the image of the invisible God" (Colossians 1:15). Only in Him did the fullness of God dwell. Colossians 1:19. Only of Him could it be said that He was "the express image" of God's nature and being. Hebrews 1:3. He is the One who made the perfect covenant by His precious blood. Hebrews 8:6-13; 9:14-28. Only He was able to teach the will of God with a unique authority. Matthew 5—7. Only He lived a perfectly sinless life. Hebrews 4:15. Only He is a perfect exhibit of what it means to walk in *agape* love, overcoming evil by meekly accepting ill treatment and injustice. I Peter 2:21-23. Only He is a perfect Example for us to follow as we also seek to walk in love and meekness. I Peter 3:8, 9; 4:1. And He is the One who will come for His saints on the last day. John 6:39, 40, 44, 54; I Thessalonians 4:13—5:4. Sound principles in interpretation require us to *seek to understand the revelation of God as Christ exhibited and taught it.*

The Old Testament Not Final

In all frankness it must be stated that the Old Testament Scriptures also contain various laws and regulations for Israel which seem not to reflect the full light of Christ and His redemptive love. (And is this not precisely what one would expect in pre-Christian times?) Israel as a nation was permitted by God to wage war. Deuteronomy 7:1-31; Judg. 1:1-4. Deception was sometimes practiced. 1 Samuel 16:1. Divorce and remarriage were permitted. Deuteronomy 24:1-4. Polygamy was allowed within certain regulations—the multiple wives dared not be sisters. Exodus 21:10; Leviticus 18:18. Israel had the institution known as the avenger of blood (Numbers 35:12; Joshua 20:3)—perhaps as a limitation of vengeance to one person. As a nation, provision was naturally made for Israelites to go to law. Exodus 21, 22. Oaths were permitted. Numbers 5:19. Many crimes were punishable by death. Exodus 21:12, 15, 16, 17; 22:18, 19. Woman held a rather inferior status (Numbers 30:3-8), although vastly higher than that of the other Near Eastern peoples of that era. The general practice of the writers of the New Testament is to constantly ground their doctrine upon the holy Scriptures of the Old Testament. *The Greek New Testament* published by the United Bible Societies, second printing, 1968, contains a list of quotations of Old Testament passages in the New, *and these number about 2,500.* The New Testament writings also mark an advance over the Old Testament, for the full revelation of God had come in Christ before the writing of the New Testament books. The New Testament writers constantly make the truths of divine revelation as taken from the Old Testament more deep and penetrating. *Christ Himself set the pattern in His Sermon on the Mount.* Matthew 5-7. With what appears to be an unerring instinct (it was Holy Spirit illumination, to be sure), the apostles reach for those Old Testament passages which will make good "pilings" upon which to rest their doctrine of faith and life.

What do Christ and His apostles do, on the other hand, about those statements of the Old Testament which reflect pre-Christian attitudes and behavior? The general answer is that they simply pass over them, rather than to point out that they are not using them. Perhaps the only exception is Christ's teaching on marriage and divorce. Jesus first of all laid down the rule that marriage is binding for life. And in good New Testament form Christ grounded His doctrine in the Scriptures of the Old Testament, citing the provision for permanent monogamy from Genesis 2:24, with its law commanding to leave and cleave. He then set forth God's holy law, "What therefore God hath joined together, let not man put asunder." The Pharisees thought that they could upset the doctrine of Christ by appealing to the law of Moses; so they inquired why Moses had *commanded* to write a bill of divorcement. Jesus replied gently that Moses *permitted* divorce "because of the hardness of your hearts . . . but from the beginning [Genesis 2:24] it was not so." Then He added, "And I say unto you, Whosoever shall put away his wife, except it be for . . . [unchastity] , and shall marry another, committeth adultery: and whoso marrieth her which is put away doth commit adultery" (Matthew 19:3-12). (The Greek word here rendered *unchastity* was a broad term which could include any form of immorality, such as fornication, adultery, or incest. It was not confined to premarital unchastity as is now the common usage of the English word *fornication*.)

This explanation of Christ, as to why Moses in Deuteronomy permitted divorce and remarriage, is as far as theologians can go today in explaining the pre-Christian laws and regulations of Judaism which fall short of the standards of Christ and His apostles.

So far we have seen that we need to interpret the Bible *grammatically*, actually seeking to determine as carefully and honestly as possible what the words actually mean; we saw that we needed to take into account the *context* of any given statement; we saw that we need to get all the light which *historical research,* including *archaeology,* can throw on the Scriptures; we saw that it was important to try to understand the *fulfillment* of the old covenant by the new, and the implications of this fulfillment; and we saw that the Scriptures are to be interpreted *Christologically.* We need yet to take a brief look at what scholars such as Louis Berkhof call *theological* interpretation. What is meant by this expression?

Theological Interpretation   Goal of all interpretation which must permeate method

We may begin this discussion by reminding ourselves that it is true, both that the Bible *contains* God's Word, and also, because of its Holy Spirit inspiration, that it *is* God's Word. And since the entire corpus of Scripture may be recognized as God's Word, there is an ultimate unity to the Book which is dependent upon God Himself. In other words, *the canons of the Old and New Testament Scriptures are a divine intention.* It is agreed on all hands—by both Roman Catholic and Protestant scholars—that when Christ and the apostles refer to the Scriptures they mean the twenty-four books of the Jewish canon, our thirty-nine books. (Attwater, *A Catholic Dictionary*, p. 479; cf. p. 153.) And there is no dispute within Catholic or Protestant circles on the twenty-seven New Testament books. The authority of these New Testament books—just like the twenty-four of the Old— does not rest on ecclesiastical decree or pronouncement. They are in the canon of the church because they were inspired; they are not inspired because of any conciliar action. The twenty- seven books of the New Testament have an authority which the church recognized as *the voice of God.* This voice was heard basically in *apostolic* books, either written or dictated by apostles, or resting on their witness. (Thus Mark wrote down the preaching of Peter, while Paul was Luke's spiritual father.) *The ancient Christian Church had a lively tradition as to which books could be depended on to present apostolic truth.* (A sort of skeleton canon emerged first, evidently within the second century, while a number of the smaller books were added to the canon later. As early as A.D. 367 Athanasius listed our twenty-seven New Testament books and designated them as canonical.)

That the entire Bible is worthy of the high designation, Word of God, means that it is more than the writings of good men. It all has its ultimate source in God. This is true not only of the Old Testament prophetic writings, where holy men of God came before God's people with the declaration: "Hear the Word of Yahweh!" It is just as true of the apostolic writings, the content of which did not always come by a special revelation from God. Luke, for example, indicates that he engaged in historical research in the writing of his Gospel, being careful to look up eyewitnesses. Luke 1:1-4.

If the whole body of the Scriptures is the Word of God, it follows that there is often a divinely intended meaning in the Book beyond the conscious intention of its many writers. It is therefore the task of the Spirit-illuminated reader of God's Word to go beyond what the original hearers or readers may have understood the Word to mean; and even to go beyond what the original writers on some occasions may have meant when they wrote. *We must seek for the meaning which God Himself intends us to get from His Word.* It is He who is the God of all truth. In *regeneration* He gives us a nature akin to His own. In *illumination* He assists us to reach His intention as we read and meditate upon His Word. Theological interpretation therefore means that we must honestly seek by meditation and prayer to reach the understanding of God's Word which *He* intends us to attain. For example, the Jews of Moses' day no doubt thought that God had created the universe in six twenty-four-hour days. What Moses thought, we have no way of knowing. What God intends us to get from this account is undoubtedly how He in an orderly manner in six divine "days" brought everything into being which exists, and how He is the Creator and Sustainer of it all. Augustine (354-430), the great church leader, perceived this truth, although among the churchmen of his day his insight was not accepted. But Augustine was no doubt right in rejecting a strictly literal interpretation. Surely God does not want us to consider these as six puny earth days, but six divine "days."

Another illustration is the teaching of the New Testament apostles that Christ would come "soon." We do not know how the early church understood this word, nor how the apostles themselves meant it. And that is not the main question. The real point is, What does God want us to take from this word? Undoubtedly the answer is qualitative, rather than quantitative. He wants us to seek to live expectantly, aware that He could appear in glory at any time and deliver His church militant from all her suffering and distress; rather than to try to compute the number of days or years which will elapse until His *parousia* takes place.

A third illustration would be the animal sacrifices for sin in the Old Testament era. We now know that animal sacrifices can never atone for human sin. Hebrews 10:4. Therefore it was only by the grace of God that Israelites could have their sins forgiven. There was no intrinsic value in animal sacrifices. Yet the promise of the law was clear and unequivocal that when the people of Israel made their sacrifices, God would forgive them. Was Moses aware that these sacrifices were of value only insofar as the Israelite was penitent? Did not many Israelites think that there was something intrinsically meritorious about their cultus? Theological interpretation insists that what matters is what God wants us to understand, not how the people of the time understood His Word—or failed to understand it; nor how even the writer understood it. (And in relation to this illustration, we recall how the great prophets such as Isaiah and Amos thundered against the hypocritical manner in which many Israelites participated in the cultic worship of that era.) Similarly the Jews thought that circumcision was instituted forever; they found it hard to accept the teaching of the New Testament that God's concern is only with the "circumcision" of the "heart," that is, with the new birth which the Holy Spirit effects in each convert who turns from sin and yields to Jesus Christ as Saviour and Lord.

Christian Truth in Focus

In the interpretation of the Old Testament, the teaching of *Christ* and His *apostles* is normative. In the interpretation of the New Testament, however, it is the *Holy Spirit* who must enable us to reach God's intention. And in relation to the New Testament, *the church must seek to make central the same emphases which Christ and His apostles had.* This means that the church must preach repentance from sin and faith in the Lord Jesus Christ. Acts 20:17-35. It means making central the new birth and Christian holiness. Romans 5-8. It means seeking to do everything possible to carry out the command to witness and evangelize. Matthew 28:18-20; Acts 1-28. It means operating on the principle of love, the Greek *agape*. John 13; Romans 12, 13; I Corinthians 13; I John 1-5. The New Testament asks us to live as "strangers and pilgrims" in this wicked world (Hebrews 11:13; I Peter 2:11; Romans 12:1, 2), but it does not ask us to adopt the cultural accidents of a Palestinian first-century culture: eating the food of that period, wearing the clothing of that day, or using the means of transportation and communication of that era. There is nothing "Christian" about a given mode of life, such as being a shepherd like David of old. It is just as Christian to be a pilot on an airliner, or a researcher for a drug company, both of which are in many ways more significant in today's society. True Biblical interpretation for the Christian Church means discovering and emphasizing *the central affirmations of the Christian faith*, not distorting New Testament Christianity by majoring in minor matters, or teaching an unscriptural sacramentalism, or putting undue stress on peripheral or "occasional" elements of Scripture. (The term "occasional" refers to the obvious fact that certain instructions were one-time directives to certain individuals or groups, and not relevant in any major way for the ongoing life of the church. For example, Paul told a sensitive Timothy to use a little wine to quiet his stomach.)

This principle of interpretation could also be put negatively: *Do not distort New Testament truth.* Making Christianity into a system of ceremonies would be an example of distortion. We cannot afford to give the impression that the heart of Christianity is observing ordinances. Almost all Christians agree that baptism and the Lord's Supper are permanent practices for the church of Christ. And there is certainly nothing but commendation for such bodies as the Church of the Brethren, the Mennonites, and the Brethren in Christ, if they also practice literally the washing of the saints' feet—providing they stress in all these ceremonies (baptism, Lord's Supper, and foot washing) both the value of their literal observance and the spiritual realities of which the ceremonies are symbols. For unfortunately it is possible for people to make of religious ceremonies an end in themselves, and ceremonialism is indeed a distorted Christianity. The only way to avoid ceremonialism is by a clear and vigorous teaching program which keeps God's people aware that the ceremonies of Christianity, even baptism and the Lord's Supper, are meaningful only because they witness to the spiritual blessings which we have in Christ. The warnings of Amos and Isaiah against ceremonialism without faith and obedience are still needed! For sacramentalism dies hard, and there are still many nominal believers who think that they are recipients of God's grace through the sheer reception of the water of baptism, or the bread and cup of the Lord's Supper. But any participation in "sacraments" without faith in Christ is an abomination to God. No spiritual blessings are in the New Testament promised on the flimsy basis of trust in *ex opere operato*. The danger of a wooden literalism in the understanding of the New Testament cannot be denied. Especially serious is the error of sacramentalism, which thinks to receive blessings through the sheer observance of ceremonies.

It must be admitted also that there is no easy way to draw a line between the practices which the Lord intended to be permanent symbols and ceremonies for the church, and the first-century cultural expressions of values and virtues which were not intended by God to be kept permanently in their original form. Most Christian bodies include in the former group baptism and the Lord's Supper, and in the latter such instructions as to keep one's loins girded and to greet one another with a holy kiss. The Society of Friends denies that such a distinction can be drawn, and therefore keeps no ordinances at all, stressing only the spiritual realities of which the ceremonies are symbols. But this attitude of rejecting New Testament ordinances has been justly rejected by almost all of Christendom. Having the loins girded is properly regarded as a symbol of constant readiness [for the Lord's Return] and is certainly no instruction to the church around the globe to wear for all time the flowing garments of Palestine in the time of Paul the Apostle. There are other practices which are not so readily classified in the category of permanent symbol or temporary expression of spiritual attitudes. The symbol which comes closest to baptism and Lord's Supper is that of the basin and towel (John 13:1-17), for it must be admitted that the words of institution spoken by the Lord in John 13 sound just as binding upon His disciples as those pertaining to the bread and the cup. The basin and towel point to the obligations which membership in a redeemed brotherhood involves: the obligations of serving love, as well as symbolizing the daily spiritual cleansing which Christian believers enjoy in Christ. On the other hand, there seems to be no mention in the Acts of the literal observance of foot washing as a Christian ceremony for the church.

Sacramentalism and the giving of undue attention to the ceremonies of the New Testament are not the only way to distort the teaching of the New Testament. How frequently is it said by well-meaning believers: "I'm only a sinner, saved by grace." Now there is no doubt at all about the truth of our being saved by grace, nor about our pre-conversion state having been that of a sinner. The only question relates to the testimony, "I'm only a sinner." Does this statement ring true to the testimonies of the saints of the first century? Is it not much more the case that New Testament believers rejoice in. the consciousness that they have been "washed, . . . sanctified, . . . [and] justified in the name of the Lord Jesus, and by the Spirit of our God" (I Corinthians 6:11)? Do they not rejoice that the Lord Jesus has baptized them with the Holy Spirit, in contrast with the water baptism of John? Matthew 3:11; Acts 1:5; 2:4, 17, 38; 11:15, 16. And does not Christ's baptism with the Spirit result in the death of the old sinful life, and a subsequent walk "in newness of life" (Romans 6:4)? Was not the "old man" crucified with the Saviour on Golgotha's cross? Romans 6:6. Does not the indwelling Holy Spirit render powerless (Greek, *katargeo*) the "body of sin" (Romans 6:6)? Instead of constantly emphasizing their sinfulness, ought not the saints to "reckon" themselves as "dead indeed unto sin, but alive unto God through Jesus Christ our Lord" (Romans 6:11)? And are we not commanded not to allow sin to "reign" in our mortal body, nor to "have dominion" over us? Romans 6:12, 14. Rather, are we not even now love-servants of God, with our "fruit unto holiness, and the end everlasting life" (Romans 6:22)? Yea, "the Spirit of life in Christ Jesus" enables us to attain unto genuine righteousness. Romans 8:1-11. How utterly we deny the chorus of New Testament witnesses for holiness by emphasizing only our sinfulness and denying that possibility of victory over sin which the New Testament commands us to appropriate by faith! Just as the Spirit of God teaches us in the Book of Acts the centrality of those ceremonies which set forth our redemption in Christ, so He also wants us to grasp the reality of our deliverance from the law of sin and death as set forth in the epistles of the New Testament.

It is also possible to distort New Testament truth by constantly asserting that our only message is that of grace. It is certainly true that the believer's only hope is God's grace in Christ. We are saved by grace (Ephesians 2:8), we stand in grace (Romans 5:2), and it is by grace that we anticipate the future enjoyment of God's glory (Acts 15:11). But grace is not God's only word for us. We are also taught by our Lord that we must both hear and "do" His words. Matthew 7:24. And a faith which does not issue in good works is "dead" (James 2:26). It takes more than lip profession to enter the divine kingdom; we must also do the Father's will. Matthew 7:21. If anyone wishes to be Christ's disciple, he must deny himself, daily take up his cross [of suffering as a disciple], and "be following" his Lord. Luke 9:23. It is true that the water of life is offered to us "gratis" (as the Rheims New Testament of 1582 so well renders the Greek), but Christ also said: "Blessed are they that do his commandments, that they may have right to the tree of life, and may enter in through the gates into the city" (Revelation 22:17, 14).

One more illustration must suffice. In many Christian circles, especially those in the Arminian tradition, there tends to be a constant emphasis on faithfulness, on "holding out." And this is, to be sure, a good emphasis. It is Biblical. Only he will be saved who "shall endure unto the end" (Matthew 24:13). But this emphasis on enduring can be rightly understood only when it is related to another New Testament emphasis, namely, the assurance that it is none other than God who is able to keep His children from falling, "and to present . . . [them] faultless before the presence of his glory with exceeding joy" (Jude 24). Behind the faithful disciple, therefore, stands the infinitely more faithful God, the One who has "begun a good work" in His children, and who will certainly "perform it until the day of Jesus Christ" (Philippians 1:6). Paul knew in whom he had believed, and he was persuaded that God was able to guard his deposit "against that day" (II Timothy 1:12). Christ's "sheep" are secure because: (1) He is able to keep them, and (2) it is

His will to do so. John 10:27-29.

There is only one way for a believer to avoid distorting the truth of God's Word. That is the lifelong practice of reading constantly in the holy Scriptures, praying for Holy Spirit illumination, living up to all the light one has, ever seeking for a more perfect understanding of the divine will, heeding the warnings of God's Word, and claiming His promises. And here both the glorious doctrinal tradition of the Christian Church, as set forth in the ancient creeds, and the living teaching ministry of the church are of immense help in assisting the saints to see the truth of God's Word in good focus. Even the New Testament contains what were likely ancient confessions of faith which stress the centrality of the Lord Jesus as the object of our faith:

> HE WHO WAS
> manifest in the flesh,
> justified in the Spirit,
> seen of angels,
> preached unto the Gentiles,
> believed on in the world,
> received up into glory (I Timothy 3:16).

One of the finest hymns of the church is one which really sets forth the Christian faith in sharp focus, making central what the New Testament makes central, the catechetical hymn of Mrs. Cecil F. Alexander, 1848:

> There is a green hill far away,
> Without a city wall,
> Where the dear Lord was crucified,
> Who died to save us all.
>
> We may not know, we cannot tell,
> What pains He had to bear;
> But we believe it was for us
> He hung and suffered there.
>
> He died that we might be forgiv'n
> He died to make us good,

That we might go at last to heav'n,
    Saved by His precious blood.

There was no other good enough
    To pay the price of sin;
He only could unlock the gate
    Of heav'n, and let us in.

O dearly, dearly has He loved,
    And we must love Him too,
And trust in His redeeming blood,
    And try His works to do.

We have found him,
    of whom Moses in the law,
    and the prophets, did write,
JESUS OF NAZARETH.

4

A CHRISTOCENTRIC BIBLE

Man Spiritually Needy

To any person who takes up the Scripture and reads it with an open mind and an honest heart it soon becomes evident that the Bible contains a number of major themes. For one thing, the Scriptures uniformly recognize man's sin and need. Instead of being humbly and gratefully dependent upon God, man is by nature in a state of revolt against his Creator. Psalm 51 is a penitent confession of sin:

> Have mercy upon me, O God,
>> according to thy lovingkindness:
> according unto the multitude of thy tender mercies
>> blot out my transgressions.
> Wash me throughly from mine iniquity,
>> and cleanse me from my sin. . . .
> Behold, I was shapen in iniquity;
>> and in sin did my mother conceive me.

The prophets spoke effectively of man's depravity and sin:

> The heart is deceitful
>> above all things,
> and desperately wicked:
>> who can know it (Jeremiah 17:9)?

And this insight is found in the earliest book of the Bible, Genesis:

> "And God saw that the wickedness of man was great in the earth, and that every imagination of the thoughts of his heart was only evil continually" (Genesis 6:5).

The Lord Jesus spoke of human depravity in these pregnant words: "That which cometh out of the man, that defileth the man. For from within, out of the heart of men, proceed evil thoughts, adulteries, fornications, murders, thefts, covetousness, wickedness, deceit, lasciviousness, an evil eye [envy], blasphemy, pride, foolishness: all these evil things come from within, and defile the man" (Mark 7:20-23).

In a similar vein, the great Apostle Paul describes in Romans 1 the downward course of the human race into ever greater pollution in sin and idolatry as men lost the true knowledge of God which they originally enjoyed. And in Romans 7 the apostle confesses from personal experience how unable man is in himself to achieve that obedience to the divine law which God requires. "I know that in me," wrote Paul, "(that is, in my flesh,) dwelleth no good thing" (Romans 7:18). In desperation he cries out: "O wretched man that I am! who shall deliver me from the body of this death?" And in true Christian faith he answers his questions: "I thank God through Jesus Christ our Lord" (Romans 7:24, 25).

Yahweh Redeems

A second major emphasis of the Bible, indeed the central emphasis of the whole Scripture, is on a God who acts redemptively for the salvation of man. The Old Testament is much concerned with the history of Abraham and his seed, with the people called Israel. The man Israel, better known as Jacob, went down to Egypt from Canaan to escape a famine, possibly in the nineteenth century B.C. Four hundred and thirty years later, when his family had become a huge throng of slaves, the full twelve tribes of Israel, God with a mighty hand acted to "redeem" His chosen people from the oppression of Egypt. He brought them out under the leadership of Moses, renewed His faithful covenant with them, gave them His holy law, which Israel solemnly covenanted to keep, and eventually brought them into Canaan under the leadership of the successor of Moses, a leader named Joshua. Moses served as lawgiver and deliverer. He was the man whom God constantly used as His spokesman, and whom He directed to set up the priesthood, the sacrificial system, and the movable sanctuary, the tabernacle.

The psalmists of Israel delighted in rehearsing the history of their nation, confessing the greatness of God's creation and of His redemption, the perversity of Israel, and the steadfast love of the God of the covenant, Israel's faithful Yahweh:

> Who can utter the mighty acts
>> of the Lord [Yahweh] (106:2)?
> Happy is he that hath the God of Jacob
>> for his help,
> whose help is in the Lord [Yahweh] his God:
>> which made heaven, and earth,
> the sea, and all that therein is (146:5, 6).
> By the word of the Lord [Yahweh]
>> were the heavens made;
> and all the host of them
>> by the breath [Spirit] of his mouth (33: 6).
> When I consider thy heavens,
>> the work of thy fingers,
> the moon and the stars,
>> which thou hast ordained;
> what is man,
>> that thou art mindful of him?
> and the son of man,
>> that thou visitest him (8:3, 4)?

The great psalm on God as Creator is 136. After a threefold ascription of praise, addressing the Creator as Yahweh, as God of gods, and as Lord of lords, the psalmist continues:

> To him that by wisdom made the heavens . . .
> To him that stretched out the earth
>> above the waters . . .
> To him that made great lights . . .
>> The sun to rule by day . . .
>> The moon and stars to rule by night . . .
> To him that smote Egypt in their firstborn . . .
> And brought out Israel from among them . . .
>> with a strong hand,

and with a stretched out arm . . .

To him which divided the Red sea into parts . . .

And made Israel to pass through the midst of it . .

> But overthrew Pharaoh and his host
> in the Red sea . . .

To him which led his people through the wilderness . . .

> To him which smote great kings . . .
> and slew famous kings . . .

And gave their land for an heritage . . .

Even an heritage unto Israel his servant . . .

> Who remembered us in our low estate . . .
> And hath redeemed us from our enemies . . .

O give thanks unto the God of heaven:

For his mercy endureth for ever.

Psalm 104 is the most detailed in its beautiful description of the God of nature. And there are many references to the covenant which Yahweh made with His people, and to the giving of His law through His servant Moses, especially in Psalm 105.

> He made known his ways unto Moses,
> his acts unto the children of Israel (103:7).
> O give thanks unto the Lord [Yahweh] ;
> > call upon his name:
> Make known his deeds
> > among the people . . .
> He is the Lord [Yahweh] our God . . .
> He hath remembered his covenant for ever,
> the word which he commanded
> > to a thousand generations.
> Which covenant he made with Abraham,
> > and his oath unto Isaac;
> and confirmed the same unto Jacob
> > for a law,
> > and to Israel
> > for an everlasting covenant (105:1-10).

Psalm 105 goes on to review the history of Israel, referring to Joseph's entrance into Egypt as a slave and his rise to be a mighty

ruler, the coming of the Israelites into the same land, the great increase of the Israelites, their oppression by the Egyptians, the divine commission of Moses and Aaron, the mighty signs which Moses
performed in Egypt (that is, the plagues which made the Egyptians
willing to allow the exodus of Israel), the guidance of the cloud by
day and the fire by night, the mighty ways God supplied the needs
of Israel: quail, "bread from heaven" [manna], and water from the
rock, and how He finally brought them into the "lands of the
heathen," that is, Canaan. The Israelites had a vivid memory of
their national history and of God's mighty redemptive acts in their
behalf. Yahweh was for them *the God of history.* He was the One
who acted for His chosen people. The line of redemptive history
began with Abraham, Isaac, Jacob, and Joseph, and continued
through Moses, Samuel, and all the prophets who brought God's
holy Word to Israel.

Messianic Prophecy

But God was for Israel not only the One who had created
heaven and earth, and who had redeemed His elect people from the
bondage of Egypt; He was also the One who from the very beginning spoke in a veiled manner, especially at first, of a future
Redeemer, a Messiah, who would bring in the divine kingdom in
great fullness and blessing. The number of references to this Redeemer and the Messianic Age were at first few and mysterious,
but as the centuries rolled around the prophets spoke more and
more plainly about Him—His birth, His Spirit-filled ministry, His
suffering and death, and the spiritual blessings of His reign. The
Messianic hope began quite dimly, to be sure. Genesis 3 contains
this mysterious word:

> And I will put enmity
> between thee and the woman,
> and between thy seed
> and her seed;
> it shall bruise thy head,
> and thou shalt bruise his heel (3:15).

Were Genesis 1-3 devoid of depth meanings, we would conclude that the passage has to do with the incessant strife of the human race with serpents. But if one reads the entire corpus of Scripture, it becomes evident who the "serpent" of Genesis 3 really was, and who the "Seed" of the woman was who would conquer the "serpent" [by a mighty act of redemption on Golgotha]. The tempter was none other than "the dragon, that old serpent, which is the Devil, and Satan" (Revelation 20:2).

Another veiled reference to this "Seed" is found in several references in Genesis to the means of universal blessing which Israel would be to the world. In connection with Abraham's divine call to leave Ur and migrate to an unknown land, God said in another mysterious word:

> And I will make of thee a great nation,
> and I will bless thee,
> and make thy name great;
> and thou shalt be a blessing:
> And I will bless them that bless thee,
> and curse him that curseth thee:
> and in thee shall all families of the earth
> be blessed (Genesis 12:2, 3).

The Apostle Paul, having been a devout Jew, one who knew and loved the sacred Scriptures, was keenly aware of this promise to Abraham. And so convinced was Paul of the continuity of our blessings in Christ with God's redemptive acts in the Old Testament era, that he was able to describe Christian salvation as "the blessing of Abraham," and as "the promise of the Spirit" (Galatians 3:14). The promises, continues Paul, were made to Abraham "and his seed"— which a Hebrew exegete would certainly have interpreted to mean the posterity of the patriarch. But not so Paul. Paul uses the Old Testament Christologically. He literally sees Christ everywhere. And so he makes a Christological application here. He writes: "He saith not, And to seeds, as of many; but as of one, And to thy seed, which is Christ" (Galatians 3:16).

The woman's Seed will conquer the tempter. Abraham's Seed will be a means of universal blessing. Another obscure word was spoken by the Lord through Balaam, that strange and vacillating prophet of Moses' day:

> I shall see him,
>> but not now:
>
> I shall behold him,
>> but not nigh:
>
> There shall come a Star out of Jacob,
> and a Sceptre shall rise out of Israel . . .
> Out of Jacob shall come he
> that shall have dominion . . . (Numbers 24:17, 19).

And almost as obscure was the word of the dying Jacob to his son Judah:

> The sceptre shall not depart from Judah,
> nor a lawgiver from between his feet,
>> until Shiloh come [or, until he, whose it is, come] ;
>> and unto him
>
> shall the gathering of the people be (Genesis 49:10).

Less obscure, and yet rather awesome, were the solemn words of God through His great prophet, Moses:

> I will raise them up a Prophet
>> from among their brethren,
>> like unto thee,
>
> and will put my words
>> in his mouth;
>> and he shall speak unto them
>
> all that I shall command him.

> And it shall come to pass,
>> that whosoever will not hearken
>> unto my words which he shall speak in my name,
>
> I will require it of him (Deuteronomy 18:18, 19).

Through His servant Nathan the prophet, the Lord assured King David: "And thine house and thy kingdom shall be established for ever before thee: thy throne shall be established for ever" (II Samuel 7:16). Who was this mysterious King, this son of David, who was to have a reign without end? (Or was it perhaps to be a continuing dynasty?) The great prophets of the Old Testament look forward in the Spirit to One who would occupy the throne of David:

> For unto us a child is born,
>> unto us a son is given:
> and the government shall be upon his shoulder:
> and his name shall be called
>> Wonderful Counsellor,
>> The mighty God,
>> The everlasting Father,
>> The Prince of Peace.
> Of the increase of his government and peace
>> there shall be no end,
>> upon the throne of David,
>> and upon his kingdom,
>> to order it,
> and to establish it with judgment
>> and with justice
> from henceforth even for ever.
> The zeal of the Lord of hosts
>> will perform this (Isaiah 9:6, 7).
> Behold, the days come, saith the Lord,
> that I will raise unto David
>> a righteous Branch,
>> and a King shall reign and prosper,
>> and shall execute judgment and justice
>>> in the earth.
> In his days Judah shall be saved,
> and Israel shall dwell safely:
>> and this is his name
>> whereby he shall be called,
> THE LORD OUR RIGHTEOUSNESS (Jeremiah 23:5, 6).
> But they shall serve the Lord their God,
>> and David their king,
>> whom I will raise up unto them (Jeremiah 30:9).

Somehow this "David" will be a royal person, as well as some sort of spiritual Shepherd:

> And I will set up one shepherd over them,
>> and he shall feed them,
>> even my servant David;
> He shall feed them,
> and he shall be their shepherd.
> And I the Lord will be their God,
>> and my servant David
>> a prince among them;
> I the Lord have spoken it (Ezekiel 34:23, 24).

The days of this "David" will follow a time of political and spiritual trouble:

> For the children of Israel shall abide many days
>> without a king,
>> and without a prince,
>> and without a sacrifice . . .
> Afterward shall the children of Israel return,
>> and seek the Lord their God,
>> and David their king;
> and shall fear the Lord and his goodness
>> in the latter days (Hosea 3:4, 5).

Once again, this Messiah shall somehow be both priest and King:

> Behold the man whose name is the BRANCH;
>> and he shall grow up out of his place,
>> and he shall build the temple of the Lord . . .
>> and he shall bear the glory,
> and shall sit and rule upon his throne;
> and he shall be a priest upon his throne . . . (Zechariah 6:12,13).

Some sort of tragedy involving "piercing" will come to this royal priest:

> And I will pour upon the house of David,
> and upon the inhabitants of Jerusalem,
>> the spirit of grace
>> and of supplications:
> and they shall look upon . . . [Him]
>> whom they have pierced . . . (Zechariah 12:10).

This mysterious figure in Hebrew prophecy would therefore in some sense be both a King, occupying the "throne of David," and a Priest, serving as a spiritual Shepherd over His people. And somehow He would be "pierced." But that is not all. There is a strange person depicted in the latter part of the prophecy of Isaiah, the "servant of the Lord," a figure who will suffer severely, even unto death, and in some mysterious way His suffering will be vicarious in character. He will suffer in behalf of the sins of His people. And in some unknown manner His ministry will extend in a special way to the Gentiles:

> Behold my servant, whom I uphold;
> mine elect, in whom my soul delighteth;
>> I have put my spirit upon him:
>> he shall bring forth judgment to the Gentiles . . .
> I the Lord have called thee in righteousness,
>> and will hold thine hand,
>> and will keep thee,
> and give thee for a covenant of the people,
>> for a light of the Gentiles;
>> to open the blind eyes,
> to bring out the prisoners from the prison,
> and them that sit in darkness
>> out of the prison house (Isaiah 42:1, 6, 7).
> He is despised and rejected of men;
>> a man of sorrows,
>> and acquainted with grief:
> and we hid as it were our faces from him;
>> he was despised,
>> and we esteemed him not.
> Surely he hath borne our griefs,
>> and carried our sorrows:
> yet we did esteem him stricken,
>> smitten of God,
>> and afflicted.
> But he was wounded for our transgressions,
> he was bruised for our iniquities:

the chastisement of our peace was upon him;
and with his stripes
we are healed.
All we like sheep have gone astray;
we have turned every one to his own way;
and the Lord hath laid on him
the iniquity of us all . . .
He shall see of the travail of his soul,
and shall be satisfied . . . (Isaiah 53:3-6, 11).

It may be noted that in none of the prophecies cited thus far has
the title "Messiah" appeared. As a matter of fact, the word itself is
rare in the Old Testament, and when it is used it generally refers to
an earthly king, who was often spoken of as God's "Anointed" or
Messiah. (The Greek word, *Christ,* is the exact equivalent of the
Hebrew title, *Messiah.*) And although there are but few instances in
the canonical Scriptures of the Old Testament in which Israel's coming Prophet-Priest-King figure is designated as the Messiah, the
Messianic hope was strong and clear among the Jews as the New
Testament era dawned. When Herod the Great (who died in the
spring of 4 B.C.) learned from the Wise Men of the birth of a Jewish
king, he called together the chief priests and scribes of the Jews and
demanded of them where the Christ (Messiah) should be born. They
were able to report confidently that His birth was to take place in
Bethlehem, "for thus it is written by the prophet" —whereupon
they quoted from Micah: "But thou, Bethlehem Ephratah, though
thou be little among the thousands of Judah, yet out of thee shall he
come forth unto me that is to be ruler in Israel . . . " (5:2). In a similar manner, the Samaritan woman assured the Lord Jesus that she
was aware that the Messiah was to come, and that He would teach
them all things. John 4:25. On the other hand, the Jews seem to have
overlooked those passages which refer to the deity of the Messiah,
such as that His name was to be Immanuel [God is with us] , a
clear reference to the divine Word becoming flesh in the incarnation. Isaiah 7:14. Also the Jews were puzzled (John 12:34) when
Christ picked up the lofty Messianic title, Son of Man, from Daniel
7:13— that heavenly figure who appeared before the Ancient of days,

And there was given him
>   dominion, and glory, and a kingdom,
that all people, nations, and languages,
>   should serve him:
his dominion is an everlasting dominion,
>   which shall not pass away,
and his kingdom that which
>   shall not be destroyed (Daniel 7:14).

On the other hand, Peter did make his great confession at Caesarea Philippi in Messianic terms: "Thou art the Christ [Messiah], the Son of the living God" (Matthew 16:16). And yet even Peter had failed to note the most important use of the title, "Messiah," in the Old Testament: "Know therefore and understand, that from the going forth of the commandment to restore and to build Jerusalem unto the Messiah the Prince shall be seven weeks, and threescore and two weeks. . . . And after threescore and two weeks *shall Messiah be cut off*, but not for himself . . ." (Daniel 9:25, 26). At that time Peter held to the "son of David" and "throne of David" prophecies for the Messiah, but he did not understand that the Messiah was to be *pierced* (Zechariah 12:10), and to be *cut off* (Daniel 9:26). All through the ministry of Christ, popular expectation was that the Messiah was to "restore again the kingdom to Israel"— to use the phrase which the apostles employed with the risen Christ (Acts 1:6)—that is, to throw off the yoke of Rome and set up a Messianic kingdom similar to that of the Maccabees. For whatever reason, the Messianic hope of the Jews had no place for the fulfillment of the Suffering Servant of Isaiah; the Jews saw the Messiah as a political deliverer, not a spiritual redeemer.

Christ Fulfills the Old Testament

To some extent the saving acts of God in the New Testament era corresponded to His redemptive acts in the period of the Old Testament. Moses was marvelously spared death in a time of compulsory infant exposure, and grew up with a splendid training for his role as the national redeemer of his people. Similarly, John the Baptist had a remarkable birth, being born according to the divine Word to an aged couple. And the Redeemer of the world, also according to a divine Word, was conceived of the Holy Spirit and born of the Virgin Mary. And just as God enabled Moses to perform attesting "signs" (miracles) in connection with his ministry in ancient Israel, so the Lord Jesus performed many "signs" in confirmation of His divine commission as the incarnate "Word" of God: healing the sick, restoring sight to the blind, casting out demons, and even raising the dead—so that He could say to Philip: "Believest thou not that I am in the Father, and the Father in me? the words that I speak unto you I speak not of myself: but the Father that dwelleth in me, he doeth the works. Believe me that I am in the Father, and the Father in me: or else believe me for the very works' sake" (John 14:10, 11).

There are yet other parallels between the Old and the New Testament eras. Old Testament Israel experienced national redemption from the bondage of Egypt, while the church of Christ experienced spiritual redemption from the bondage of sin through the crucified and resurrected Lord Jesus. Israel of old had at its head the twelve patriarchs, the sons of Jacob. The new Israel had at its head the twelve apostles of Christ. The old covenant was ratified by the sprinkling of blood on the book of the covenant and on the covenanting people. The new covenant was ratified by the blood of the eternal Son of God, shed on Golgotha's cross. Atonement for sin in the period of the Old Testament was made by animal sacrifices—although it was only by the grace of God that forgiveness was extended to obedient worshipers who came to the tabernacle with their animal sacrifices. Atonement for sin was made once and for all by the Lord Jesus when He "through the eternal Spirit offered himself without spot to God" (Hebrews 9:14).

The New Testament opens on a strong spiritual note, the message of spiritual redemption. The angel told Joseph to call the name of the Child, *Jesus*—a symbolic name, "Saviour"—for He it is who "shall save his people from their sins" (Matthew 1:21). And the birth of this Saviour is declared to be a fulfillment of the prophetic word: "Behold, a virgin shall be with child, and shall bring forth a son, and they shall call his name Emmanuel, which being interpreted is, God

with us" (Matthew 1:23). And when the angel Gabriel informed
Zacharias of the coming birth of John, he stated that he would "be
filled with the Holy Ghost. . . . And many of the children of Israel
shall he turn to the Lord their God . . . to make ready a people prepared for the Lord" (Luke 1:15-17). Likewise the angel Gabriel,
when making the holy annunciation to Mary, assured her that the
name of her Son was to be Jesus, that God would give Him the
throne of David, that He would reign over the house of Jacob forever, and that He should be called the Son of God. Luke 1:31-35.
When John was born, Zacharias was filled with the Holy Spirit and
spoke out the praises of the Lord, rejoicing in the coming ministry of
John which he saw as faithfulness on the part of God to the holy
covenant He had made with Abraham. God had, said Zacharias,
raised up a horn of salvation for His people, He would grant deliverance from Israel's enemies, and John would "be called the prophet
of the Highest [God the Most High] : for thou shalt go before the
face of the Lord to prepare his ways; to give knowledge of salvation
unto his people"—and here it becomes clear that this salvation is a
spiritual deliverance from sin, not a national deliverance from a foreign overlord—for Zacharias defined this salvation as "the remission
of their sins" (Luke 1:67-79). Similarly the aged Simeon, filled with
the Holy Spirit, had received the revelation that he should not die
until he had seen the Lord's Christ. And when he saw Him, he described Him as,

> A light to lighten the Gentiles,
>
> and the glory of thy people Israel (Luke 2:32).

About three decades later, when John began his ministry, he
proclaimed, not political deliverance, but repentance from sin, and
the necessity of bringing forth "fruits worthy of repentance" (Luke
3:8). And Jesus defined His own Messianic ministry in His sermon at
Nazareth by quoting from Isaiah 61:

> The Spirit of the Lord is upon me,
>
>> because he hath anointed me
>>
>> to preach the gospel to the poor;
>
> he hath sent me
>
>> to heal the brokenhearted,

> to preach deliverance to the captives,
> and recovering of sight to the blind,
> to set at liberty them that are bruised,
> to preach the acceptable year of the Lord
>
> (Luke 4:18, 19).

All through the ministry of Christ, particularly in His suffering and death, the writers of the four Gospels recalled one passage after another in the Scriptures of the Old Testament that the Christ event reminded them of. Christians accept the explanation of this phenomenon which the Lord gave predictively in His great discourses immediately preceding His arrest, trials, and death. He promised the apostles that the Holy Spirit would enable them to remember His words (John 14:26), that the Spirit would take the things of Christ and reveal them to the apostles (John 16:12-15). *It was therefore the Holy Spirit who constituted the apostles as reliable witnesses to the words and deeds of Christ, and trustworthy interpreters of the Christ event.*

When we turn to the canonical Gospels, we find the writers, especially the apostles Matthew and John, stressing the fulfillment of the Old Testament Scriptures by the Lord Jesus. He was the Messiah because He fulfilled the Messianic prophecies. Indeed the whole Old Testament tended to mirror the Gospel events as recorded and interpreted by the apostles. Matthew sees even the flight of the holy family to Egypt as the fulfillment of prophecy, for the prophet Hosea had written: "Out of Egypt have I called my son" (Matthew 2:15)! Even more remarkable is the way Matthew makes a play on words as he quotes the prophecy about the "Branch" of the stem of Jesse: NZR one of the words for "Branch" in Hebrew, has the first three consonants of Nazareth! Matthew 2:23. Christ's removal from Nazareth to Capernaum fulfilled Isaiah's prophetic word relating to "Galilee of the nations":

> The people which sat in darkness
> saw great light;
> and to them which sat in the region
> and shadow of death
> light is sprung up (Matthew 4:14-17).

The healing ministry of Jesus was interpreted by Matthew as the fulfillment of Isaiah's prophecy:

> Himself took our infirmities,
>
> and bare our sicknesses (Matthew 8:17).

Likewise Matthew saw in the loving and tender ministry of the Lord Jesus the fulfillment of the prophecy of Isaiah 42. Matthew 12: 17-21. And Matthew records that Christ Himself appealed to Isaiah in support of His use of parables. Matthew 13:14, 15.

The Apostle John was especially active in pointing to Old Testament statements which paralleled or mirrored events in Passion Week. John thought of that remarkable Messianic psalm, Number 22, as he wrote the story of the crucifixion. He pointed out that the casting of lots for Christ's tunic fulfilled the Scripture,

> They parted my raiment among them,
>
> and for my vesture did they cast lots (John 19:24).

The failure of the soldiers to break the legs of Christ also fulfilled a verse which in the Old Testament related to the Passover lamb, "A bone of him shall not be broken" (John 19:36). And the soldier's spear thrust into the side of Christ fulfilled Zechariah's prophecy, "They shall look on him whom they pierced" (John 19:37). Even the resurrection of the Lord was mirrored in the Old Testament, for Psalm 16 states:

> For thou wilt not leave my soul in *Sheol;*
>
> neither wilt thou suffer thine Holy One
>
> > to see corruption (interpreted in Acts 2:29-33; cf. John 20:9).

The Book of Acts is most rewarding for its record of how the apostles interpreted the Old Testament Christologically. The treachery of Judas was described in a Psalm of David. Acts 1:16. The propriety of choosing a successor to Judas had a Scriptural foundation. Acts 1:21. The gift of the Holy Spirit on the day of Pentecost was predicted by Joel the prophet. Acts 2:16-21. David predicted the resurrection of the Christ. Acts 2:25-31. Christ's ascension and enthronement at God's right hand reflect Psalm 110:1,

> Yahweh said unto my Lord,
>
> > Sit thou at my right hand,

until I make thine enemies
thy footstool (cited, Acts 2:34).

(Incidentally, Psalm 110:1 is the Old Testament prophecy most often alluded to or quoted in the Scriptures of the New Testament.) That the Messiah should be a suffering One was, declared Peter, revealed by God through "the mouth of all his prophets" (Acts 3:18). Heaven must receive this Christ until the times of restitution [restoration] of all things, "which God hath spoken by the mouth of all his holy prophets since the world began" (Acts 3:21). Judging by the explanatory verses which follow, it appears that Peter is referring to the full bringing in of the Messianic kingdom and its blessings which will come to completion only at the triumphant return of Christ on the Last Day:

"For Moses truly said unto the fathers, A prophet shall the Lord your God raise up unto you of your brethren, like unto me; him shall ye hear in all things . . ." (Acts 3:22, 23, citing Deuteronomy 18).

Peter boldly went on: "Yea, and all the prophets from Samuel and those that follow after, as many as have spoken, have likewise foretold of these days. Ye are the children of the prophets, and of the covenant which God made with our fathers, saying unto Abraham, And in thy seed shall all the kindreds of the earth be blessed. Unto you first God, having raised up his Son Jesus, sent him to bless you, in turning away every one of you from his iniquities" (Acts 3:24-26). It would be difficult to find a stronger apostolic witness to the Christocentric nature of the Old Testament Scriptures than this word from Peter, the dean of the Twelve.

In rebuking the unbelieving Jewish leaders, Peter cited Psalm 118:22, identifying the crucified Christ with the "stone which the builders refused," and alluding to Christ's exaltation as the One who "is become the head of the corner" (Acts 4:11). Indeed the Spirit-filled Christians with one accord lifted up their voice in praise to their Creator-God, and cited Psalm 2 as predicting the passion of the Christ: Herod, Pilate, the Romans, and the Jews did only what God had all along intended—they made possible the redemption of the world through the atoning death of the Lord's Christ (Acts 2:24-28), fulfilling the word which God spake through David "by the Holy

Spirit" (as the oldest manuscripts read in Acts 4:25).

The Book of Acts contains a number of examples of apostolic sermons which summarize the *kerygma*, the proclamation of the Christ event; chapter 10 is a good example. After proclaiming how God anointed Jesus, and how Jesus went about doing good—of which holy life the apostles were God's witnesses—Christ was put to death "on a tree," only to be resurrected by God and presented to His chosen witnesses, "even to us, who did eat and drink with him after he rose from the dead. And he commanded us to preach unto the people, and to testify that it is he which was ordained of God to be the judge of quick and dead." Then Peter added a most significant word: "To him give all the prophets witness, that through his name whosoever believeth in him shall receive remission of sins" (Acts 10:34-43).

An even fuller account of Paul's sermon at Pisidian Antioch is given in Acts 13. Paul began his message with God's election of His people Israel; he continued with God's mighty deliverance in the exodus of Israel from Egypt; and gradually Paul worked through his summary of Old Testament history to the time of David, a man after God's "own heart"; and, from David, the apostle leaped to the Christ, saying: "Of this man's seed hath God according to his promise raised unto Israel a Saviour, Jesus." Paul then recounted the history of Israel's wicked unbelief which put Jesus on the cross in the days of the procurator Pilate, which crucifixion took place because of Jewish blindness to the Messianic import of the Old Testament Scriptures: "They knew him not, nor yet the voices of the prophets which are read every sabbath day." In referring to the crucifixion, Paul remarked: "And when they had fulfilled all that was written of him, they took him down from the tree, and laid him in a sepulchre. But God raised him from the dead. . . ." Paul also declared that Christ's resurrection fulfilled Psalm 2: "Thou art my Son, this day have I begotten thee"; also Isaiah 55, "I will give you the sure mercies of David"; and Psalm 16, "Thou shalt not suffer thine Holy One to see corruption." Finally Paul warned his hearers to hearken to the prophetic warning against despisers. Acts 13:16-41.

And just as Peter and Paul grounded their proclamation of the

Gospel of Christ upon the prophetic Word of the Old Testament, so James the Lord's brother appealed to the words of the prophet Amos to explain what was happening in the first century of the Christian era. James explained that the Lord was gathering from the Gentiles "a people for his name," and in so doing He was rebuilding David's tabernacle. Acts 15:13-21.

Luke reports that before His ascension, Christ discoursed with Cleopas and his companion as the three of them made their way by foot from Jerusalem to Emmaus. When Christ discovered how blind they were to the Christocentric character of the Old Testament, He exclaimed: "O . . . [foolish men], and slow of heart to believe all that the prophets have spoken: Ought not [the] Christ to have suffered these things, and to enter into his glory? And beginning at Moses and all the prophets, he expounded unto them in all the scriptures the things concerning himself" (Luke 24:25-27). And in the same vein Christ addressed ten of His apostles: "These are the words which I spake unto you, while I was yet with you [before my crucifixion], that all things must be fulfilled, which were written in the law of Moses, and in the prophets, and in the psalms [the first and largest book of the third part of the Hebrew canon], concerning me. Then opened he their understanding, that they might understand the scriptures, and said unto them, Thus it is written, and thus it behoved [the] Christ to suffer, and to rise from the dead the third day: and that repentance and remission of sins should be preached in his name among all nations, beginning at Jerusalem. And ye are witnesses of these things" (Luke 24:44-48).

Christ's illuminating summary of the Christocentric character of the Old Testament must have caused the hearts of the ten apostles to "burn" just as did His exposition to Cleopas and his friend. Luke 24:32. Furthermore, Christ continued with His teaching program during the forty days of His post-resurrection life on earth. Acts 1:3. The significance of all this is that *the Christocentric interpretation of the Old Testament came ultimately from the lips of the Lord Jesus Himself.* Further development of this principle of interpretation may have come from the Holy Spirit as the apostles meditated through the years on the significance of the Christ event, and as they read the Scriptures of the Hebrew canon with an alert eye for passages with Messianic import or application. The Christian faith could therefore be summarized by Paul as belief in "all things which are written in the law and in the prophets" (Acts 24:14). And in Romans Paul states that the Gospel was "promised afore [beforehand, in advance] by his prophets in the holy scriptures." He defines the content of the Gospel as "His Son Jesus Christ our Lord," who was "made of the seed of David according to the flesh; and declared [designated, set forth] to be the Son of God . . . by . . . [His] resurrection from the dead" (Romans 1:1-4). With a little fuller statement Paul wrote elsewhere about the Gospel in these words: "For I delivered unto you first of all that which I also received, how that Christ died for our sins according to the scriptures" (I Corinthians 15:1-4).

This is the Christ who in the Gospels is addressed as the "Son of David." In the Acts He is the One "whom God raised from the dead." In the epistles He is "Jesus the Lord." And in the Book of Revelation, He is "the prince of the kings of the earth" (1:5), the One "clothed with a vesture dipped in blood" (19:13). "And he hath on his vesture and on his thigh a name written, KING OF KINGS, AND LORD OF LORDS" (19:16). Revelation also assures us that "the testimony of Jesus is the spirit of prophecy" (19:10): that is, all that God's servants, the prophets, have to tell us centers in the Lord Jesus Christ, the One of whom Moses, the prophets, and the other Biblical authors wrote.

> *Ecce homo: Christus Victor!*
> [Behold the Man: Christ the Victor!]

5
TRANSMISSION AND TRANSLATION

One of the most fascinating aspects of Biblical scholarship is the story of the preservation, textual modification, and scholarly restoration of the texts of the Old and New Testaments. Let us look at each of the Testaments in turn. The Hebrew Old Testament was a long time in being written. From the time of Moses to the day of Malachi and Ezra was a millennium of time. In a general way we may say that, considering its great age, the text of the Old Testament books has been well preserved. We have a number of lines of transmission from before the time of Christ which we may compare with one another. First, what might be called the "official" Jewish text of the Old Testament is known as the Masoretic text. It is the traditional Hebrew text delivered to us by the Jewish copyists of the Middle Ages, the so-called Masoretes. The manuscripts of this text are remarkably uniform, including the small amounts of textual error which had crept into the text over the millennia of time in which the manuscripts were copied by hand. Second, we have the text preserved in the Greek Version of the Old Testament, known as the Septuagint. Third, we have the Samaritan Pentateuch. And fourth, we now have the text preserved in the Dead Sea Scrolls.

Nature of Textual Variants

What is the nature of these minor textual variations? First of all, it must be recalled that in the ancient Semitic languages the copyists did not bother to write vowels; only the consonants were put down.

Thus Psalm 23:1 would have appeared in Hebrew letters, corresponding to our English: "Th Lrd s m shphrd (I) shll nt wnt." Some five to eight centuries after Christ, Jewish scholars added vowel points to the consonantal text, little marks above, between, and below the consonants, indicating the vowels which traditionally were understood as going with the consonants of each word. When we compare the Hebrew words which are thus formed with the sense of the Hebrew words which by inference stand behind the Greek Old Testament known as the Septuagint, it is evident that the Septuagint sometimes associated other vowels with the consonants of the manuscripts they used, as well as having an occasionally different consonantal text. This Septuagint translation from the original Hebrew was made in Egypt in the general period, 285-135 B.C. In some cases, modern scholars can restore the correct vowels, in contrast with what are believed to be the erroneous vowels of the Masoretic text, either on the basis of the Septuagint or other ancient versions, or by studying the sense and context of the passage. For example, Deuteronomy 28:22 speaks in the Masoretic text of "*sword,* blasting, and mildew," whereas if different vowels are read with the first word, the phrase reads, "*drought,* blasting, and mildew" (compare modern versions). In a number of cases the Hebrew letters "d" and "r" are confused with each other, so that a man will be called Diphath in one place and Riphath in another. The words for *Syria* and *Edom* in Hebrew differ only as to whether the middle consonant is a d or an r. Note the parallel passages, II Samuel 8:12 and I Chronicles 18:11, where this confusion occurs: the Masoretic text reading Syria in Samuel and Edom in Chronicles (Edom is probably correct). This was of course a mistake of the eye. Other textual variants seem to have been a mistake of the ear, suggesting the likelihood that at times one person slowly dictated the text as a number of scribes made copies at the same time—an ancient effort at mass production of books! For example, the Hebrew words meaning "not" and "to or for him" are homonyms. Psalm 100:3 reads in the Masoretic text: "It is he that hath made us, and *not* we," whereas scholars believe that it originally read, "It is he that hath made us and we [belong]*to him*" (compare modern versions). Sometimes copyists recopied a part of a verse by mistake; Leviticus 20:10 may be such a case: "And the man that committeth adultery with another man's wife . . . that committeth adultery with . . .," a mistake which later copyists evidently smoothed out by adding, "*even he* that committeth adultery. . . ." Sometimes by a sheer oversight one or more words were skipped in copying. For example, in I Samuel 13:1 the age of Saul when he began to reign is missing. The Hebrew reads, in the idiom of that tongue: "Saul was a son of year [s] in his reigning." (The translators of the Septuagint solved the problem by omitting the verse; the King James Version revisers made it read, "Saul reigned one year"—which was certainly not the meaning of the writer; the American Standard Version revisers made the conjecture that he was possibly *forty* and put the word both in italics and in brackets, and also added a marginal note indicating that it was "supplied conjecturally"; while the Revised Standard Version revisers simply indicated the missing number by the use of several periods: "Saul was . . . years old when he began to reign." A comparison of the Masoretic text of the Hebrew, which we have in our Hebrew manuscripts, with the Hebrew text which inferentially underlies the Greek Version of the Old Testament, indicates that the same Hebrew letters were occasionally divided up into different words. Bruce M. Metzger points out that this is like dividing the following letters: GODISNOWHERE into two different combinations of words: "God is now here," and "God is nowhere" *(Text of the New Testament,* p. 13). Finally, it must also be confessed that some changes were made deliberately, the motives being religious in character. For example, Israelites sometimes named their children after *Baal:* note the case of the man who was named *Eshbaal* in I Chronicles 9:39. Later copyists were heartily ashamed of such a name, and sometimes substituted *Bosheth* (shame) for *Baal,* making the same man *Ishbosheth* (II Samuel 2:8). Compare also *Jerubbaal* (Judges 6:32) with *Jerubbesheth* (II Samuel 11:21). Finally, mention should be made of the fact that a number of mistakes were made in the copying of numbers (e.g., II Samuel 10:18; I Chronicles 19:18).

Scholars tell us that the evidence indicates that the consonantal Hebrew text was fairly well established or standardized by at least

200 B.C., and fully so by A.D. 200. The Dead Sea Scrolls generally confirm this standardized text. Indeed, the Dead Sea Scrolls not only confirm the substantial accuracy of the Masoretic text of the Middle Ages; they also generally support the Masoretic text in comparison with the Hebrew text used by the translators of the Septuagint. There are exceptions, of course; in some cases the Septuagint, as well as the Latin Vulgate of Jerome (made by Jerome largely in the last two decades of the fourth century A.D.), seems to preserve a more accurate reading than is found in the Masoretic text. Such a case is I Samuel 14:41, which read thus originally:

"Therefore Saul said, 'O Lord God of Israel, *why hast thou not answered thy servant this day? If this guilt is in me or in Jonathan my son, O Lord God of Israel, give Urim; but if this guilt is in thy people Israel*, give Thummim.' And Jonathan and Saul were taken, but the people escaped." An ancient copyist's eye missed the words between the first and last occurrences of *Israel*, which we have cast in italic type to make the mistake more evident. The deficient text then read in Hebrew, "O Lord God of Israel, give TMM"—and the later Jewish scholars took the three consonants, TMM, to stand for the Hebrew word, TAMIM ("perfect"), hence the rendering: "Give a *perfect* [lot] !" (But TMM really meant *Thummim.*)

Any student of the Bible can soon discover for himself something of the nature of textual variants by studying parallel passages in the Old Testament. The following pairs of passages are more or less parallel: Joshua 15:15-19 and Judges 1:11-15; Psalm 14 and Psalm 53; Psalm 18 and II Samuel 22; Psalm 40:13-18 and Psalm 70; Psalm 57:7-11, and 60:5-12 and Psalm 108; Isaiah 2:2-4 and Micah 4:1-3; II Kings 18:13—20:19 and Isaiah 36—39; II Kings 24:18—25:30 and Jeremiah 52; II Chronicles 36:22, 23 and Ezra 1:1-3a; Ezra 2:1—3:1 and Nehemiah 7:6—8:1. Any scholarly work on Old Testament introduction will give much more detail than has been presented here; for example: Bleddyn J. Roberts, *Old Testament Texts and Versions* (University of Wales Press, 1951), and Julius A. Bewer, *The Literature of the Old Testament* (Columbia University Press, revised edition, 1922). It may be noted in passing that Bewer's uncritical adherence to classic Wellhausianism is now hopelessly out of date.

Efforts to Restore the Text of the Old Testament

We indicated earlier that by A.D. 200 the Hebrew consonantal text had about approached its final form. It is said that about A.D. 125 Rabbi Aqiba had attempted unsuccessfully to create an official standard text of the Hebrew Scriptures. About A.D. 600 the Codex Hillel was such a standardized text, but unfortunately, it is no longer extant. It appears that another effort to create a standard Hebrew text was made about the eighth century A.D., but again we have no exemplar of this text. About A.D. 975 a Jewish scholar, Aaron ben Asher, produced a fine text of the Hebrew Old Testament after many years of labor. The famous Leningrad Hebrew manuscript of the Old Testament of A.D. 1008, now designated as "L" represents the ben Asher rescension. There was also a ben Naphtali rescension, but in the opinion of the great Jewish authority, Maimonides (twelfth century), the ben Asher type of text was superior. The traditional Hebrew Masoretic text assumed its final form in the fourteenth century, only about a century before the invention of printing.

Printed Hebrew Bibles

The first printed Hebrew Old Testament was issued by the famous Soncino Press in Lombardy, Italy, in the year 1488. Unfortunately, however, it was not a good ben Asher text. Indeed, until the year 1936 the printed Hebrew Bibles were basically the text of Jacob ben Chayim, published originally, 1524-25. Ben Chayim desired to use a good ben Asher text, but he did not find the manuscripts containing such a text. He had to use late and inaccurate manuscripts. In 1936, however, for the third edition of the famous Kittel Hebrew Bible, Paul Kahle finally used Hebrew Manuscript "L" of A.D. 1008. But scholars such as Albright and Orlinsky tell us that the critical apparatus of the 1936 Kittel Bible was carelessly prepared; it contains many errors. Orlinsky reports that to date about 800 manuscripts of the Hebrew Bible have been studied. *(Introduction to the RSV Old Testament,* p. 26.)

Old Testament Textual Criticism

How do the scholars of today attempt to restore the original text of the Old Testament? First of all, they study the extant Hebrew manuscripts. Then they turn to the Samaritan Pentateuch (which has had an independent line of transmission since long before the Christian era); to the manuscripts of the Greek Old Testament, the Septuagint; to Jerome's Latin Vulgate; and to other ancient versions such as the Syriac. The Dead Sea Scrolls, which began to come to light in the late 1940's, have now been studied for almost two decades, and as we observed earlier, although they eliminate with one stroke the errors of over a thousand years of copying they confirm the remarkable carefulness of the Hebrew copyists, even before the beginning of the Christian era and ever since. Modern translators of the Old Testament use as their basic text the modern Kittel Hebrew Old Testament, but they also keep a sharp eye on the Septuagint, especially when it is supported by the Old Latin Version (second century A.D.), by the Syriac (second or third century A.D.), and by the Latin Vulgate of Jerome (end of the fourth century). Incidentally, there are no less than 8,000 manuscripts of the Latin Vulgate in existence. And the Vulgate is second only to the Septuagint in importance. It is the Septuagint which is most frequently quoted in the books of the New Testament.

The Restoration of the Text of the New Testament

When we come to the text of the Greek Testament, we have an abundance of evidence. And this fullness of manuscript evidence stands in sharp contrast with many other documents of antiquity. In his definitive study, *The Text of the New Testament*, Bruce M. Metzger points out, for example, that for the first six books of the *Annals* of Tacitus, but one lone manuscript has survived, and that of the ninth century A.D. The *Epistle to Diognetus* also survived in a single copy, only to perish by fire in 1870! For the New Testament, on the other hand, there are about 5,000 witnesses to the Greek text: 25 ostraca (pieces of pottery on which poor people inscribed portions of Scripture or other writing); 250 "uncial" manuscripts (written in capital letters) prior to the tenth century A.D.; 2,646 minuscules (written in a flowing hand from the tenth century until the fifteenth century, when printing was invented in Europe); 1,997 lectionaries (manuscripts for the public reading of the Scriptures in worship services); and 76 papyri (fragments or portions of the New Testament written on ancient papyrus paper). There are about fifty complete manuscripts, while the remaining 4,900 contain smaller or larger portions of the New Testament.

In contrast with the manuscripts of the Hebrew Old Testament, the bulk of which read almost identically—minor mistakes included—there are numerous variations in the manuscripts of the Greek New Testament, especially in those of the first centuries. Scholars must somehow therefore make a comparative study of these 5,000 witnesses in an effort to discover how the several variant readings crept into the text. What do the textual critics find as they examine these ancient manuscripts? The first major observation is that the younger (that is, later) manuscripts read very much alike. So similar, for example, are the manuscripts from the tenth century onward, that Editor A. Souter employed a single symbol to designate the "mass of the cursives" (minuscule manuscripts): a small Greek *omega*. Further study points to the fourth century A.D. as the period in which this standardized text emerged. (This situation is immensely different from that of the Old Testament, for in the Hebrew manuscripts we have generally only the type of text which became standardized, the pre-standardized types of text not being available to today's scholars.) New Testament critics therefore pore over the manuscripts which have been preserved from the second to the early fourth centuries, before a more or less uniform text arose. As they make this tedious comparison of ancient manuscripts, textual critics can formulate the principles which were followed in the creation of the common text of the Middle Ages.

Before attempting to list the principles followed in the fourth century revision of the text of the New Testament, let us make note of some technical names. First of all the standardized text of the great bulk of the minuscules is now commonly called *Byzantine* (from Byzantium, the old name for Constantinople); in the latter nineteenth century it was called the Syrian text. It seems to have originated at Antioch in Syria. The revision is sometimes ascribed to the martyr Lucian of Antioch, a famous presbyter and theologian who died in 312, although he was no doubt assisted by other scholars. Regardless of who was responsible, we do know with certainty that by about A.D. 380 the so-called Byzantine text was becoming dominant in Constantinople, the center of the Eastern Greek-speaking church. And the type of readings common in Byzantium gradually became the dominant readings of the manuscripts copied from the fourth to the eighth centuries. And from then on the pre-Byzantine readings are hardly ever found.

Three major types of pre-Byzantine readings are found in the ancient manuscripts. (1) One type of text seems to have been common in Egypt, and is often referred to as the *Alexandrian* type of text; the great textual critics, Brooke Foss Westcott (1825-1901), professor at Cambridge, and from 1890 bishop of Durham, and Fenton John Anthony Hort (1828-92), also a professor at Cambridge, thought so highly of this type of text that they labeled it "Neutral," a rather overly enthusiastic evaluation, no doubt. It is represented by the two greatest fourth-century manuscripts, Codex (a manuscript made in book form, not that of a scroll) Vaticanus or "B," and Codex Sinaiticus or Aleph. Codex 33, a minuscule commonly known as the Queen of the Cursives, often agrees with Codices B and Aleph, as do the Coptic versions, and the Scriptural citations of such writers as Clement and Origen. In the great majority of cases, modern textual critics follow the readings of these two great manuscripts, B and Aleph. (2) The family perhaps somewhat inaccurately named the *Western* text is represented in Codex Bezae or D, the Old Latin manuscripts, and in the Scriptural quotations of such ancient writers as Irenaeus, Tertullian, and Cyprian, as well as the Old Latin Version. It sometimes deviates rather sharply from the readings of other manuscripts, with striking additions and/or omissions. This rather "wild" type of text was found fairly widely across the ancient church; it was not just in Italy and Gaul, as the name "Western" might suggest. (3) The third type of pre-Byzantine text has been called the *Caesarean* and is found in certain families of minuscules such as Family 1 (the consensus of manuscripts 1, 118, 131, and 209) and Family 13 (manuscripts 13, 69, 124, 230, 346, 543, 788, 826, 828, 983, 1689, and 1789), as well as in Papyri 45, 46, and 47. It is represented also in the Armenian and Georgian versions, and in the writings of such fathers as Eusebius of Caesarea: scholar, historian, theologian, and bishop (c. 260-340).

Modern textual critics agree almost to a man that to construct the most accurate text of the original New Testament which we possibly can, we need to study the pre-Byzantine readings and by comparing them discover what the original readings were. Yet the older versions of the Bible in all European languages rest upon the Byzantine type of New Testament text. How did this happen?

Printed Greek Testaments

The scholar who printed the first common Greek New Testament was a Dutchman, Geert Geerts, commonly known by his Latin name, Desiderius Erasmus, who taught at Cambridge and who died in 1536. When commissioned by the Basel publisher, Johann Froben, to prepare an edition of the Greek Testament for publication, Erasmus rushed through a manuscript without bothering to try to collect and compare even the oldest Greek manuscripts which would have been available to him. Indeed he seems not to have used more than half a dozen in all, and he actually relied mostly on two manuscripts of about the twelfth century. His manuscript of Revelation was defective, and so he translated from Latin into Greek the last six verses of the book, a translation which contains Greek words not found in a single manuscript of the New Testament! He also translated into Greek a few other passages which he did not find in his Greek manuscripts, such as Paul's question in Acts 9:6: "And he trembling and astonished said, Lord, what wilt thou have me to do?" In 1516 Froben issued this Erasmus New Testament, a diglot, containing his *Byzantine* text of the Greek Testament, plus his own additions from the Vulgate (!), and his own Latin Version of the New Testament. Many people grumbled about the changes, particularly the omissions, from the Latin Version of the New Testament, for it deviated in various places from the familiar readings of the Vulgate, hallowed as they were by eleven centuries of church use. People also attacked the 1516 printed Greek Testament of Erasmus for not printing in Greek certain verses which they were familiar with in the

Vulgate: especially I John 5:7. This verse reads: "For there are three that bear record in heaven, the Father, the Word, and the Holy Ghost: and these three are one." Erasmus of course did not print them for good reason. They were not found in the Greek manuscripts. So he felt free to make a rather rash promise: he said he would add them to the next edition of his Greek Testament if they could be found in a single Greek manuscript. Sure enough, such a manuscript was "found" in time to be incorporated in the third edition of the Erasmus New Testament, 1522. (It is now thought likely that this manuscript was actually prepared, rather than found, in order to force Erasmus to keep his word, which he did.) In subsequent editions, after further study, Erasmus deleted this addition, however.

A Paris printer, Robert Estienne, commonly known as Stephanus, began to publish Greek Testaments in 1546. He followed largely the text of the Erasmus Testament. The third edition of Stephanus, 1550, became the more or less standard text of the Greek New Testament in the English-speaking world for almost three centuries, and therefore underlies all the older English versions. It even came to be called the *Textus Receptus* (received text), which seemed to almost put a halo over it. In other words, our King James New Testament is ultimately based largely on two late Greek manuscripts of about the twelfth century, plus some additions from the Vulgate.

Bruce M. Metzger tells us that it was a German scholar, Johann Jakob Griesbach (1745-1812), who laid down initially the basic principles of New Testament textual criticism. Griesbach issued three major editions of the Greek New Testament: Halle, 1774-77; Halle and London, 1796-1806; and Leipzig, 1803-7. But the real giants in the field came in the nineteenth century: the German scholar, Constantin von Tischendorf, whose eighth critical edition of the Greek New Testament was published, 1869-72; Westcott and Hort, *The New Testament in the Original Greek*, 1881-82 (representing twenty-eight years of scholarly research); and Bernhard Weiss, Greek New Testament, three volumes, Leipzig, 1894-1900. Since 1898 theological students commonly use the small Greek New Testament edited by Eberhard Nestle for the Württemberg Bible Society, which since 1901 gives for the most part the consensus of the readings of the critical editions of Tischendorf, Westcott and Hort, and Weiss. The twenty-fifth edition of this Nestle New Testament was published in Germany in 1963. Meanwhile the British and Foreign Bible Society kept reprinting the Nestle edition of 1904 until the new Kilpatrick edition was issued in 1958.

New Testament textual critics, as we saw earlier, are agreed that the Byzantine text is a deliberately edited text of the fourth century, and that it is reliable only insofar as it reflects pre-Byzantine readings, especially those of the *Alexandrian* type of text. As we saw, the two most massive exemplars (for the most part) of this type of text are the manuscripts *Vaticanus* and *Sinaiticus*. Indeed it has sometimes been conjectured that both of these might have been included in the fifty handsome Bibles made upon order of the Emperor Constantine in A.D. 331. We may at least declare with confidence that they are very like the fifty. Tischendorf may have been a bit too proud of his beloved *Sinaiticus* which he found at the Monastery of St. Catherine at Mount Sinai, and Westcott and Hort may have slightly overevaluated the "Neutral" text of *Vaticanus* and *Sinaiticus*, but it is today recognized that these scholars, especially Westcott and Hort, laid down in the nineteenth century principles of textual criticism which were remarkably enduring and sound.

How do textual critics account for the *Byzantine* text? It was a text which "corrected" parallel accounts to make them harmonize more fully. It added a few words here and there to make thought transitions more smooth. It selected the readings which seemed to reflect the best Greek usage when there was a choice in the pre-Byzantine manuscripts. If combining readings was a possibility, the fourth-century revisers often made such combinations. We shall shortly seek to illustrate these principles in actual studies of the text. Let it here be emphasized however that these editorial principles are not farfetched hypotheses, but are based squarely on the evidence.

Symbols Employed

In giving manuscript evidence it was long ago found convenient to have quick and convenient ways of designating major manuscripts. The foundations of this system of nomenclature were laid down by a Swiss scholar, J. J. Wettstein, in the middle of the eighteenth century (1751-52). He decided to use capital letters for the relatively few uncial manuscripts (both Roman and Greek capitals are used) and Arabic numerals for the minuscules or cursives. In 1908 an American, Caspar R. Gregory, who served as a professor at the University of Leipzig, slightly revised the Wettstein system in his scholarly work, *Die griechischen Handschriften des Neuen Testaments* (The Greek Manuscripts of the New Testament). Papyri are now designated by an Old English P, followed by a small numerical exponent, *e.g.*, 𝔓 ⁴⁵.

Basic Principles of New Testament Textual Criticism

We may also observe that textual critics of today are increasingly eclectic, not relying exclusively on any one manuscript nor even on any family of manuscripts. Textual critics make a fresh study of each textual problem, bringing to it a vast array of information, some of which is confusing and difficult. Metzger *(op. cit.,* p. 219) quotes the jovial remarks of the British scholar, A. E. Housman, who commented that the textual critic cannot go about his work like an astronomer studying the motions of the planets; he is, said Housman, much more like a dog hunting fleas! It is necessary to go after the fleas, not by a neat formula based on area studies and population figures, but rather to pursue them one by one! Nevertheless, there are some rules of thumb which do serve as genuine guides to the textual critic. (1) It is generally acknowledged that greatest weight is to be given to the ancient Greek manuscripts, rather than to later manuscripts of the Greek Testament. (2) The ancient Greek manuscripts also take precedence over the versions and the patristic citations. (3) It is also assumed that it is more likely that a scribe would lengthen a statement in an effort to strengthen it, rather than to shorten it: hence the canon, Adopt the shorter reading! (4) Likewise it is evident that it is much more likely that a scribe would try to "improve" a somewhat obscure statement, rather than to take a simple and clear one and make it more difficult: this principle leads us to still another canon of textual criticism: Adopt the harder reading! (5) If evidence is so divided as to make it very difficult to choose between readings, some weight should be given to the reading which is more characteristic of the style and vocabulary of the writer. (6) Finally, that reading should be adopted which best explains the origin of the other variants.

Sample Textual Studies

Following the *Textus Receptus* (Byzantine text), the King James Version reads thus in Matthew 6:4: "And thy Father which seeth in secret . . . shall reward thee openly." Most modern versions omit the adverb, *openly*. Why this change? The Greek adverbial phrase for "openly" is found of course in the mass of the cursives (symbol: small *omega* in Greek), as well as in the uncials L, Delta, Pi, and W. But it is omitted by the great uncials B, Aleph, Z, and the 1-family of the minuscules. If we classify the evidence by pre-Byzantine families, it is as follows: the phrase is omitted by the *Alexandrian* witnesses. B, Aleph, and Z; by the *Caesarean* 1-family; and by *Western* D. The fact that an occasional uncial manuscript contains the phrase points to its having been an ancient gloss. Some scribe, no doubt, with the most pious intentions, thought he could strengthen the promise by indicating that God would *openly* reward the almsgiver! The Byzantine revisers included the gloss because it was the fuller reading. But modern textual critics omit it because: (1) the better pre-Byzantine manuscripts omit it; (2) shorter readings are to be preferred to longer ones; and (3) it is easier to account for the longer variant by assuming that it was originally not included, than to account for the shorter reading on the basis that some early scribe would have struck it out. It should of course be clear that textual critics are *not removing* verses or words from the Bible; rather, they are discarding *glosses* which were in ancient times *added* to the Bible.

In Mark 13:33 the *Textus Receptus* (and the older English Versions, of course) reads: "Take ye heed, watch and pray." Modern versions have a shorter admonition: "Take ye heed, watch!" In this case the manuscript evidence is not overwhelmingly decisive. The added command to pray is found in the mass of the cursives and in manuscripts A and C (which commonly have Byzantine readings in the Gospels); in Alexandrian Aleph, and L, and in the Coptic versions, Sahidic and Bohairic; as well as in the Caesarean 1-family and 13-family. On the other hand, it is omitted in the best single manuscript, the Alexandrian B, and this omission is supported by the Western D and the Old Latin Version. The fact that the Alexandrian manuscripts are arrayed against each other (B to omit, and Aleph to include), and that Caesarean evidence is weighted against Western witnesses, makes the decision less easy than some textual problems are. Yet, (1) the general superiority of B over Aleph, supported by (2) the canon of the shorter reading, tips the scales in favor of its omission: as it was actually omitted both by Nestle in his Greek Testament, and by the RSV revisers. (The American Standard Version included, "and pray," but added a marginal note: "Some ancient authorities omit, *and pray*.")

John 1:18 contains a difficult textual problem. Should the text, in referring to Christ, read, "the only Son," or "the only God"? The *Textus Receptus* has what would be called the "easier" reading, *Son*. This is the reading of Manuscript A, which, as we observed earlier, has many Byzantine readings in the Gospels. But the Caesarean 1-family has "Son" also, as do some Old Syriac version manuscripts. (The Old Syriac is regarded as, "a local text of Edessa.") In favor of "God" are the great Alexandrian witnesses, B and Aleph, as well as L and Minuscule 33 ("Queen of the Cursives"); and so is C, which often contains Byzantine readings in the Gospels (but here it does not); and "God" is also the reading of the Caesarean *Thēta*. Which reading is therefore to be preferred? (1) God is certainly the harder reading, and this is a point in its favor. (2) It seems entirely reasonable for John to have written "God" in 1:18 in view of what he wrote in 1:1. (3) It is most unlikely that a scribe would have changed Son to God, but the opposite change is easily explained. (4) The manuscript evidence is stronger for God, especially in view of the agreement of B and Aleph, and in view of the support of C, of 33, and of *Thēta*. Nestle was on solid ground when he put "God" *(Theos)* in his Greek Testament. The ASV and the RSV probably erred in choosing "Son." (In Acts 20:28, "church of God" is likewise to be preferred to "church of the Lord.")

If we remember Housman's flea illustration, it will be easier for us to face the fact that the canon of the shorter reading is not one hundred percent reliable. For there is such a thing as a copyist's accidental omission. Such a case is found in Acts 4:25. Here the best manuscripts read, "Who by the mouth of our father David thy servant didst say *by the Holy Spirit*." This last phrase, "by the Holy Spirit," is, strangely enough, omitted in the *Textus Receptus*, and therefore is also not in the King James Version. But in all sincerity it must be stated that the evidence for the inclusion of these words is overwhelming. A ninth-century manuscript, P, omits them. But they are found in the Alexandrian witnesses, B, Aleph, A, Minuscule 33, in the Coptic versions; also in Western D and the Latin versions; also in the Caesarean Armenian Version, as well as in the Syriac. The omission of the phrase was evidently a sheer accident in transmission. The words are clearly and decisively genuine. (This is a good example of the honesty of textual critics, for they added to modern Greek texts and to modern versions these words which are lacking in the *Textus Receptus*, even though generally it is the shorter readings which are preferred. In this case the actual objective manuscript evidence was so strong that the theoretical principle of the shorter reading had to be rejected.)

Let us look also at an example of a combined reading in the Byzantine text. In Galatians 4:7 Paul addresses the Christian believer as God's son, and adds, according to some manuscripts, "also an heir through God." This reading is supported by Papyrus 46, by original Aleph (which means, thus it read before a later corrector changed it), by B, by A, by original C, by 33, by the Bohairic version of the Coptic, and by the citations in various church fathers. On the other hand, some manuscripts read, "an heir through Christ," rather than, "God." This reading is found in the Sahidic version of the Coptic, for example. The combined reading of the *Textus Receptus*, "an heir of God through Christ," is found in D, in a few ancient fathers, and in the mass of the cursives. Also some of the great uncials, such as Aleph and C, were "corrected" by devout scribes to this "conflate" (combined) reading. It is obvious that the weight of the manuscript evidence falls heavily to the side of the reading, "an heir through God," which is the reading of both the ASV and the RSV. But the *Textus Receptus*, of course, followed the usual canon of the Byzantine revisers in such cases; it adopted a conflate reading: "an heir of God through Christ."

We ought to look at one larger passage, that of the woman taken in adultery, and printed in our King James Version as John 7:53—8:11. (There is only one other long passage in question, the so-called long ending of Mark, 16:9-20.) This account of the adulterous woman is found in only one ancient manuscript, the somewhat erratic Codex D. It is omitted by such great Alexandrian witnesses as B, Aleph, L, and 33; by the Byzantine N and W, and by almost every ancient manuscript. Furthermore the Greek style and vocabulary deviate sharply from that of the Fourth Gospel. In the inferior and late manuscripts which have the story at all, it is found in various locations in John's Gospel, and even in Luke. The church father Augustine (354-430) was familiar with the account, and suggested that it was removed from the Gospel out of prudery. But the textual evidence is decisive that it never was a part of the Fourth Gospel. Biblical scholars believe, however, that the account is true, for as Bruce M. Metzger so well puts it, it has "all the earmarks of historical veracity" (*op. cit.*, p. 223). He labels it, "a piece of floating tradition" (p. 224). (Those who wish to devote further study to the matter of the textual criticism of the New Testament might well secure the informative lucid monograph of Sir Frederic Kenyon, *Our Bible and the Ancient Manuscripts*, as well as the special monographs of Bruce M. Metzger and J. H. Greenlee. See Bibliography.)

The English Language

Now for a quick look at the English language and the fascinating story of how God's Word was put into the English tongue. Long before the time of Christ a Celtic people lived in the British Isles and practiced the Druid religion. This religion held to immortality, along with some sort of transmigration; it involved human sacrifices, divination, and a pantheon of gods. The Druids culled the mistletoe. These Celts eventually called themselves Britons, and the land later came to be known as Great Britain.

In the first century B.C., in the years 55, 54, and 43, the Romans invaded Britain and built forts and roads. The Romans also occupied the land for four and a half centuries, until A.D. 410, when Rome's difficulties at home compelled withdrawal to the Continent.

In the fifth century A.D., a generation after the withdrawal of the Romans, the native Britons were having difficulties with the Picts and the Scots from the north, and from Saxon pirates on the southeast. The Saxons belonged to the Teutons or Germanic peoples, just as did many other tribes. One of these tribes, the Jutes, offered to assist the Britons. Around the year 449 the Jutes settled in Kent. This must have encouraged the Saxons, for three waves of them settled in England in the years 477, 493, and 530, forming three Saxon communities known as Sussex (South Saxony), Wessex (West Saxony), and Essex (East Saxony), respectively. Finally there were two waves of a third German tribe, the Angles, in A.D. 527 and 547. It was the Angles who gave their name to Britain, for eventually it became known as Angleland, or in shorter form, England. The language today which most resembles the tongue of these German tribes who settled in England from 449 to 547 is perhaps the ancient Frisian tongue of the Netherlands. The Angles, Saxons, and Jutes belonged to the West Germanic peoples, and within that category to the Low Germans of North Germany. (It was a Saxon, Martin Luther, who was the great reformer and Bible translator of Germany a thousand years later.)

The history of the English language is commonly divided into three great blocks: Old English (really Anglo-Saxon), A.D. 450- 1100; Middle English, 1100-1500 (subdivided into Early Middle, 1100-1250, Norman Middle, 1250-1400, and Late Middle, 1400-1500); and Modern English, 1500 to the present. (The name, Norman Middle English, refers of course to the enrichment of the language by the migration of the Normans from France to England in the eleventh century [1066]. The writings of Chaucer, for example, are in Norman Middle English.)

This quick introduction to English means that the language was originally a form of ancient German. This explains the great similarity between many German words and their English "cousins," which mean the same thing, or have a similar meaning. Compare, for example, such pairs of words as: *Hand,* hand; *Fuss,* foot; *Ofen,* oven; *stuhl,* stool, *Finger,* finger; *Nase,* nose; *Ohr,* ear; *Mann,* man; *Feder,* feather; *Haus,* house; *Schuh,* shoe; *Haar,* hair.

The Good News Comes to Britain

The full story of the introduction of Christianity to England is not known. It would appear that it arose quietly, probably through individual Christians who settled in the land and told the good news of Christ. In the early fourth century, three English bishops attended the Council of Arles in France. The famous Saint Patrick brought a fresh infusion of Christianity (a non-Roman Christianity) to Ireland in the fifth century. After the German tribes had populated the eastern portion of Britain, Pope Gregory of Rome in the year 597 sent a missionary to Kent, a man named Augustine. This missionary succeeded in winning the king of Kent to the Roman faith, and Augustine in turn became the first Archbishop of Canterbury. Kenneth Scott Latourette says the reconversion of Britain was practically completed in the seventh century.

Caedmon to Wyclif

Today we take it for granted that where Christianity goes, the Bible goes. But the Bible of Roman Christianity was a Latin Bible, and the Anglo-Saxons of England were of course Germanic-speaking. Unfortunately, much of the story of the role of the Bible in the history of the Christian Church in England is lost in the mists of the unwritten past. We do have little candles of light at various points, however. For example, it appears that the Lord raised up an illiterate stable boy in the seventh century, a man named Caedmon, who took the early Bible stories, as well as end-time events, and sang of them in what is called Celtic Saxon, in North England. Someone would read the material to him from the Latin Scriptures, and he took the material and made Saxon song paraphrases of the stories of Genesis, Exodus, and Daniel; of Christ's resurrection, ascension, and second coming; and of heaven and hell.

We know of five other efforts to get God's Word from Latin into Old English: (1) Around A.D. 700 Bishop Aldhelm translated the Psalms into Anglo-Saxon. (2) About a generation later the "Venerable Bede" translated the Gospel of John into Anglo-Saxon, finishing his dictation, tradition says, on his deathbed (A.D. 735). (3) About 875 King Alfred arranged to have the Ten Commandments and certain laws from the Pentateuch, as well as the Psalms, put into Anglo-Saxon. (4) A priest named Aldred made an interlinear translation of the Gospels into Anglo-Saxon, around A.D. 950. (5) Finally, an abbot named Aelfric made another Anglo-Saxon version of the Gospels about A.D. 1000.

In the period of Early Middle English we have two major known efforts at English versions of parts of God's Word. A man named Orm made a metrical paraphrase of the Gospels and Acts about A.D. 1215; it was known as the *Ormulum*. And about the middle of the thirteenth century an anonymous English translation of the Psalms was made.

In Norman Middle English there were also two more known efforts at parts of an English Bible: About 1320 someone made another version of the Psalms in the West Midlands dialect. And about twenty years later Richard Rolle made a version of the Psalms in the dialect of North England. All this amounted to five versions of the Psalms, three of the Gospels, and one of Acts in the period from the coming of the Angles and Saxons (450-550) until the year 1380. Unfortunately printing from movable type had not yet been invented in Europe; so all of these versions existed only in expensive handwritten manuscripts.

Now we come to the first great Bible translator in the history of the English Bible, John Wyclif (c. 1320-84). A man of genuine Christian faith, Wyclif was a professor at Oxford University and a pioneer reformer of the Roman church in England. Indeed he is called the Morning Star of the Reformation. With the help of an able corps of assistants, led by Nicholas de Hereford, Wyclif managed to get the whole Bible into Late Middle English. Unfortunately, like all his predecessors, Wyclif translated from the Latin Vulgate, and a poor text at that. And his version was, by modern standards, a rather poor translation. Yet it was the whole Bible, and so far as we know, the first complete manuscript Bible. After his death, his disciple, a gifted scholar named John Purvey, revised the entire manuscript, substantially improving it. B. V. Westcott, the great textual critic of the Greek New Testament, examined 170 manuscripts of the Wyclif Version, and 137 of them were of the Purvey version, while but 33 were of the original version. It is thought that Wyclif's New Testament was made about 1380, and the Old Testament followed about two years later. But the earliest extant manuscript was made in the year 1408. Wyclif wrote in the language of Middle England, not North or South, and his language has a fair admixture of Norman French. It is rather difficult for us today to read even Purvey's Version. The Wyclif-Purvey story of the prodigal son begins:

"A manne had twei sones; and the yonger of hem seide to the fadir, Fadir gyve me the porcioun of cattel, that fallith to me. And he departide to hem the catel."

A scholarly edition of the entire Wyclif Bible was published by two British scholars, Josiah Forshall and Frederick Madden, after twenty-two years of labor, *The Holy Bible*, 4 volumes (Oxford, 1850). The New Testament had been printed by John Lewis in 1731, was reprinted by Henry Baber in 1810, and was included in the Bagster Hexapla in 1841. A fine edition of the Wyclif New Testament (Purvey revision) was edited by Walter W. Skeat and published by the Clarendon Press, 1879. See further, B. F. Westcott, *History of the English Bible*, p. 21. This book has been a real help in the preparation of the present treatment on the history of the English Bible. See also the admirable monograph of F. F. Bruce, *The English Bible, A History of Translations from the Earliest English Versions to the New English Bible* (New York: Oxford University Press, 1961).

Although Wyclif died in the fellowship of the Roman Church, Archbishop Thomas Arundel spoke of him in the severest terms as, "that pestilent wretch . . . the son of the old Serpent . . . who had completed his iniquity by inventing a new translation of the Scriptures" (H. S. Miller, *General Biblical Introduction*, fourth edition,

1947, p. 329). In 1408 the Convocation of Canterbury, led by this same Archbishop Arundel, forbade all unauthorized translations of the Scriptures into the vernacular. And twenty years later, in 1428, in conformity with the decision of the Council of Constance, 1415, and by order of the anti-pope, Clement VII, the bones of Wyclif were burned as of a heretic, and the ashes thrown into the Swift River. But the distribution of English Bibles was to be resumed on a scale undreamed of less than a century later.

From Tyndale to the Bishops' Bible

The man whom God raised up to make His Word available in good English was William Tyndale (c.1484-1536). Born a century after Wyclif's death, Tyndale was a well-educated man, a master of seven languages: Hebrew, Greek, Latin, Italian, Spanish, "Dutch" (German), and English. He came upon the scene at a propitious moment. Printing had been invented in Europe a generation before he was born, and great progress had been made in the study of Hebrew and Greek. The first Greek grammar was published in 1476, a Greek lexicon in 1480, and Erasmus' Greek New Testament in 1516; the Hebrew Old Testament was printed in 1488, a Hebrew grammar in 1503, and a Hebrew lexicon in 1506. Tyndale earned his BA degree at Oxford about 1508, and his MA three years later. He also studied under Erasmus at Cambridge. When he discovered how hostile the English prelates were toward the Scriptures in the vernacular, he went to Germany to continue with his work. He arranged with a Cologne printer to get out his English New Testament, 1525, but had to flee, with the portion which had been done, to Worms, where it was quickly finished. These English New Testaments were then smuggled into England, where they enjoyed a ready market.

Tyndale was a good scholar and for the first time translated the New Testament from the original Greek into Modern English. He kept one eye on the Wyclif Version, no doubt, and constantly looked at the Latin Vulgate, the new Latin Version of Erasmus, and Luther's German New Testament. The 1525 edition was good; and the 1534 revision was excellent. Tyndale set the style for all subsequent English Bibles. Westcott found that about 84 percent of the language of *Ephesians* in the King James Version was Tyndale's, and 90 percent of *I John*. Tyndale also set to work on the Hebrew Old Testament, and completed about half of it, although only a portion of that half got into print before his death. Tyndale fell into the hands of his opponents in 1535, and after sixteen months in the Vilvorde prison, eighteen miles from Antwerp, he was strangled and burned at the stake, October 6, 1536. It is reported that at the stake with a loud voice he cried to God, "Lord, open the King of England's eyes."

Soon Miles Coverdale (1488-1569) revised Tyndale's New Testament, and the portion of the Old Testament which he had published, and completed the Old Testament. In 1535 Coverdale published the first complete printed English Bible. He leaned hard on Luther's New Testament. Westcott found, for example, that three fourths of Coverdale's changes from Tyndale's text of *I John* were based on Luther. In the Old Testament Coverdale leaned on the Zürich German Bible. It is sometimes said that Coverdale showed little originality. Yet it is also true that he showed fine discrimination as a reviser. His renderings were smooth, rather than slavishly literal. For example, where Tyndale spoke of "pride of goods," Coverdale changed it to, "pride of life."

Why was Coverdale able to publish this Bible? For one thing, Thomas Cranmer had become the Archbishop of Canterbury, and he seems to have labored tactfully to persuade King Henry VIII to take a more favorable attitude toward an authorized English Bible. In any case, Coverdale managed to get the Bible printed on the Continent (it bore the date, October 4, 1535), and that fall it went on sale in England, even while Tyndale was languishing in his Belgian prison. And even more surprising is the way Tyndale's final prayer was answered. In the second edition of the Coverdale Bible, 1537, appeared the notice that it was published, "with the King's most gracious license" (H. S. Miller, *op. cit.*, p. 347). Coverdale placed this "Protestant" note over the apocryphal books of the Old Testament:

> *Apocripha*. The bokes and treatises which amonge the fathers of old are not rekened to be of like authorite with

the other bokes of the byble, nether are they foūde in the Canon of the Hebreu.

In 1537 appeared another English Bible, often called the Matthew's Bible from the possible pseudonym, Thomas Matthew, which the editor, John Rogers, placed at the end of the dedication. Rogers was the friend and literary executor of Tyndale. His Bible was made up as follows: The Pentateuch was a Tyndale reprint; Joshua to II Chronicles was Tyndale's unpublished manuscript; Ezra to Malachi, and the Apocrypha, were reprinted from Coverdale; and the New Testament was a reprint of the 1535 Tyndale New Testament. This Bible was reprinted in 1549, and again in 1551, but in the 1551 edition the Old Testament was Taverner's revision of Matthew's Old Testament. Queen Mary put Rogers to death in 1555.

The first really "Authorized Version" was from its size commonly known as the Great Bible. It was Coverdale's revision of the Matthew's Bible, and was printed in Paris in April, 1539. Thomas Cromwell, who was beheaded the following July, served as a sort of private sponsor of the work. King Henry VIII evidently took a liking to this Bible, and Cromwell was able to issue a royal proclamation, ordering a copy to be placed in every church, and directing that it be read publicly in each church. The proclamation also asked the clergy to "provoke, stir, and exhort every person to read the same" (H. S. Miller, *op. cit.,* p. 350). Imagine all this in less than three years from Tyndale's martyrdom! The Great Bible was popular; it passed through seven editions, 1539-41, and was again reprinted in 1550 and 1562. The edition of April, 1540, was a Thomas Cranmer edition, and the Bible was after that often called the Cranmer Bible. The Psalter of the English Prayer Book is taken from the Great Bible.

Another English Bible was published in 1539, the so-called Taverner Bible. Richard Taverner was an Oxford scholar and lawyer, and later also a minister of the Gospel. He slightly revised the Matthew Bible of 1537, and published it in London, 1539, dedicating it to Henry VIII. This Bible did not influence later revisions of the Coverdale Bible as much as it deserved to. Words like *verity* and *advocate* in the Tyndale tradition, Taverner changed to *truth* and *spokesman. Similitud* became *parable* in Taverner's Bible, and *whelpes* became *dogges*. On the other hand, he changed Tyndale's *nynty & nyne* to *iiij score & xix!*

Queen Mary, a vigorous Roman Catholic, came to the throne of England in 1553, and by putting about 300 Protestants to death won the nickname, Bloody Mary. Some of the Protestants of England fled to Geneva during her reign, and one of them, William Whittingham, a scholar who was married to Calvin's wife's sister, made a revision of the Tyndale New Testament of 1535, and published it in 1557. Whittingham was a man of great learning, and he did a fine job. Other scholars then got to work on an entire Bible, revised Whittingham's revision of the Tyndale New Testament, and for the Old Testament made a revision of the Great Bible. The outstanding Hebraist of the group was Thomas Sampson. Another member of the revision committee was none other than Coverdale, who also was in Geneva for his health, attempting to escape the fate of Cranmer, Latimer, Ridley, and Rogers. Still another reformer in exile was John Knox, and he too helped to produce the Geneva Bible of 1560. John Calvin wrote the Introduction. Queen Mary died in 1558 and was succeeded by her half sister Elizabeth. The Geneva Bible was dedicated to Queen Elizabeth. It became very popular, passing through over 160 editions, and was even a serious competitor for a time with the King James Version, which appeared sixty-one years later. The last printing of the Geneva Version was in 1644. The Geneva Bible was the first to be printed with Roman type, with verse division, with the omission of the Old Testament Apocryphal books, and with italic type for words supplied by the translators to complete the sense.

The second Authorized Version was the so-called Bishops' Bible of 1568, a revision of the Great Bible made by a committee which included a number of Anglican bishops. The Geneva Bible influenced the 1568 revision, especially in the books of the prophets. The revision committee was instructed to avoid any bitter notes—a fault which many translators and revisers were then guilty of—to mark the genealogies and other places "not edifying," so that readers could omit the reading of them, and to replace any words offensive to good taste. There were twenty editions between 1568 and 1606; no more were made after the publication of the King James Version. The Bishops' Bible was far less popular than the Geneva Version with its 160 editions.

The Authorized Version of 1611

For hundreds of years now *the* English Bible has meant the King James Version. It was the third Authorized Version. The occasion for its preparation was the dissatisfaction of the Puritans with the available English Bibles. King James I of England attended a conference held at Hampton Court the middle of January, 1604, to consider the matters which the Puritans considered "to be amiss" in the Anglican Church. A Puritan, Dr. John Reynolds, president of Corpus Christi College, Oxford, made the proposal that a new version of the English Bible be prepared. The idea was not generally very well received, but for some reason, King James liked it. Two professors, Dr. John Harding of Oxford and Dean Lancelot Andrewes, were to work with Bishop Richard Bancroft in making plans for the preparation of the new version. On July 22 of 1604 the king notified Bancroft that he had appointed fifty-four translators. (Forty-seven names have been preserved, two Puritans and forty-five other Anglican scholars.) It must be emphasized that this was a most distinguished panel of learned men. About 1604 the task of revision actually began. The revisers were broken into six companies as follows: Genesis to II Kings (at Westminster), I Chronicles to Song of Solomon (at Cambridge), Isaiah to Malachi (at Oxford), Old Testament Apocrypha (at Cambridge), Gospels, Acts, and Revelation (at Oxford), and the Epistles (at Westminster).

The revisers were instructed: (1) to follow the wording of the third edition (1572) of the Bishops' Bible as much as possible; (2) to retain the familiar form of Bible names; (3) to retain established ecclesiastical terminology; (4) to employ chapter and verse division; (5) to confine marginal notes to comments on the translation—that is, no doctrinal notes were to be made; (6) to insert cross references; (7) to avoid the peculiarities of the [Puritan] Geneva Version and the [Roman Catholic] Rheims New Testament of 1582; and (8) to be free in the use of synonyms for the same original Greek or Hebrew words—an instruction which was indeed fully followed!

After each company had completed its assigned books, an overall Committee of Twelve, two from each company, was to review and revise the whole manuscript. Finally Bishop Thomas Bilson of Winchester and Dr. Miles Smith were to put on the finishing touches. The Anglican bishops were to solicit the clergy for scholarly suggestions, and recognized authorities were to be consulted by mail.

After several years of toil and labor the new revision rolled from the presses of Robert Barker in 1611, a large folio volume printed in Old English type, with Roman type where italic type was later employed. Each chapter had an "argument" (summary) at its head. Except in the Apocrypha, each column had a folio line indicating content. In the prose sections, paragraph marks were used, down to Acts 20:28, where they inexplicably cease.

Although a few people threw dust in the air, objecting loudly to this changed Bible, it was soon popular, and in the first thirty-three years went through 182 editions. In the early years, constant revision went on: 400 improvements were made in the second edition, for example. One of the last major revisions was made by Dr. Benjamin Blayney, 1765-69, a professor at Oxford. The Ussher Chronology was added to the King James Version in 1701.

The title page of the King James Version indicates that it was "Translated out of the Original Tongues and with the Former Translations diligently Compared and Revised by His Majesty's Special Command." It would have been a little more accurate had it read, "A Revision of the Third Edition of the Bishops' Bible by a Comparison with the Original Tongues. . . ." But in any case this third Authorized Version tended to become THE Authorized Version.

Like all other versions it of course had its faults. "Strain at a gnat" (Matthew 23:24) was evidently a typographical error for, "strain out a gnat." The Greek in I Corinthians 4:4 means, "I know nothing *against* [not, *by*] myself." Somehow the period got lost after *Anathema* in I Corinthians 16:22. The verse means: "If any man love not the Lord Jesus Christ, let him be [accursed]. [Our Lord, come!]" (It was one mistake to omit the period, and another to leave the Aramaic untranslated for the English reader.) There were various points in the Old Testament which could have been improved by the help of the ancient versions. No distinction is made between the simple past (aorist) and the progressive past (imperfect) tenses of Greek verbs, and likewise the force of the present tense in the imperative and subjunctive moods, as well as in the infinitive, is ignored. Yet the King James Version was certainly the best English translation in existence when it appeared, and it has held the field well ever since. It was not until the middle of the twentieth century that the Christian Church in America began to make wide use of more modern versions.

The English Revised Version

The fourth Authorized Version was largely a failure, namely, the English Revised Version, 1881-85, sometimes called the Canterbury Revision. The British committee in 1880 consisted of thirty-six Anglicans, seven Presbyterians, four Congregationalists, two Baptists, two Methodists, and one Unitarian. (An American committee assisted them.) The ERV was made because it was felt that the English language had changed considerably since 1611 ("let" no longer meant "hindered," for example: Romans 1:13), better Greek manuscripts were available, textual criticism had developed into a science, and solid progress had been made in language studies in Greek and Hebrew. And there is no doubt about the many improvements which were actually made in the ERV. Obsolete words were replaced, and an earnest effort was made toward more uniform renderings for the same words in the original. A better discrimination was made between the original tenses, especially in the Greek. Closer attention was given to the Greek article. The Greek prepositions were also more carefully rendered. Paragraphing was added to the text. Proper names were made uniform in the Old and New Testaments. Chapter and page headings were deleted. And textual notes were made in the margins. (See H. S. Miller, *op. cit.*, pp. 373-79.) The chairman of the Old Testament Company was Bishop Browne, and of the New Testament Company, Bishop C. J. Ellicott.

Why then was the ERV largely a failure? For some reason, people liked the beauty and cadence of the Elizabethan English of the King James Version, the lovely turns of its phrases, its delightful variety in vocabulary: all this regardless of whether or no the ERV was a more scholarly and exact version. Initial sales of the ERV New Testament were phenomenal. Nearly three million copies sold in less than a year. But after the initial excitement died down, people began to return to their beloved King James Bible, and the sales of the ERV dropped sharply.

The American Standard Version

Early in the preparatory work for the ERV, the British committee decided to invite the cooperation of American scholars. Philip Schaff was entrusted with the selection of the American portion of the committee, which organized with William Henry Green of Princeton as chairman of the Old Testament committee, and Theodore Dwight Woolsey of Yale as chairman of the New Testament committee. Schaff was president of the American committee to revise the KJV. Of the original thirty-four members of the American committee, thirty served. The work of revision on the American side of the Atlantic was carried on by correspondence with the British committee. Perhaps the method of cooperation was not satisfactory. In any case, the Americans were not satisfied with the rejection of some of their revision plans. This led ultimately to the publication of the American Standard Version Bible (New Testament, 1900; entire Bible, 1901). Scholars have said many good things about the ASV: it is an improvement over the ERV, it renders very accurately the force of the original languages, and the like. The committee included some very learned men: George E. Day, for example, was secretary of the Old Testament committee, and J. Henry Thayer of the New. And the ASV did make significant advances over the KJV. The revisers took the word *Saint* out of book titles. The Paraclete is always the Holy Spirit (not Ghost). The Greek word for *Covenant* is generally so translated, rather than as *Testament*. The Greek word *diabolos* is used only in the singular, whereas there are many *demons*. The corn of the British was changed to *grain*. The definite relative was made *who* rather than *that* or *which*. But the most impressive change was perhaps the chief cause of keeping the ASV in the role of a minor version, while the KJV marched on in full domination of the market: that change was to print the proper name of God in the Old Testament (Hebrew, *Jahweh*; KJV and ERV: the LORD) as *Jehovah*. For one thing, the word "Jehovah" is itself an error. It is the consonants of *Jahweh* read with the vowels of "Lord"—a dreadful mistake linguistically. And the Christians of America did not like it. They wanted the Bible to say, "The Lord is my shepherd," not, "Jehovah is my shepherd" (Psalm 23:1). The ASV was a scholar's Bible, but it did not constitute a popular threat to the KJV.

The Revised Standard Version

The text of the ASV of 1901 was copyrighted to prevent unauthorized translations. In 1928 this copyright was entrusted to the International Council of Religious Education. This Council, in turn, appointed a committee to have charge of the text of the ASV, and to study the question of its possible revision. In 1937 the Council appointed a committee to make the revision which the earlier committee had recommended. Twenty-two scholars served on this committee: fifteen on the Old Testament committee, with Fleming James of the University of the South as executive secretary, and nine on the New Testament committee, with James Moffatt of Union Theological Seminary of New York as executive secretary. Three men served on both the Old and New Testament committees, one of them being chairman of both committees: Luther A. Weigle of Yale University. After many years of work the Revised Standard Version New Testament was published on February 11, 1946, and the RSV Old Testament on September 30, 1952. (The Apocrypha appeared in 1957.) The RSV abandons all Elizabethan verb forms (*doest, heareth*) except in prayer. Following the Septuagint, the Greek New Testament, the Latin Vulgate, and the King James Version, it uses "LORD" for the Hebrew *Jahweh*, rather than the ASV's Jehovah. It retains much of the beautiful grace and cadence of the KJV. Poetry is set in stanza form. The page has folio lines but no chapter summaries. Alternate readings are given in footnotes. There are some cross references, but no center margin. Quotation marks are used for direct quotations. There is a commendable freedom in rendering Greek words such as *de* (*now, and, but,* or omit it). Weights and measures are often given in modern equivalents. Sometimes the translation approaches, perhaps legitimately, a semi-paraphrase. (But compare the liberty also taken by the King James translators in John 13:6, where they inserted the name, *Peter.*) A most valuable contribution to the study of the history of the English versions of the Bible from Tyndale to the RSV is the eight-version New Testament, edited by the chairman of the RSV committee, Luther A. Weigle, *The New Testament Octapla* (New York, Edinburgh, Toronto: Thomas Nelson & Sons [1962]).

Five years after the publication of the RSV Bible, it was reported that the King James Version was outselling the RSV about eight to one. How is this to be accounted for in view of the many merits of this most recent revision of the Tyndale-Coverdale Bible? For one thing, the RSV and the Revision Committee were subjected to perhaps the most severe attack which had ever been made on a Bible version or its revisers. The committee members were accused of doctrinal unsoundness, and the version was attacked as if the King James Version were the absolute standard, and any deviations from it were wicked errors. (For many Christians, any change in the wording of the English Bible is disturbing.) Even more amazing, the RSV was sharply condemned for the same features which were accepted without comment in other versions! After some years, however, the furor began to die down, and the RSV began to increase greatly in stature and use. In 1952 the three boards of the Mennonite Church (education, missions, and publication) appointed a committee to prepare a critical evaluation of the new version. The committee, Harold S. Bender, Chester K. Lehman, and Millard C. Lind, issued in 1953 a careful and judicious report which was reprinted in 1964: *The Revised Standard Version, An Examination and Evaluation* (Scottdale, Pennsylvania: Herald Press).

It is indeed a long way from the slavish English version of the Vulgate, made by Wyclif, to the scholarly and well-polished Revised

Standard Version. But we may be sure that the Holy Spirit is able to use any version of His Word in the vernacular to bring the Word of life to hungry souls, and to lead penitent sinners to Jesus Christ as Saviour and Lord.

Other Recent Versions

This brief survey will not take up the efforts of Roman Catholics, of Jews, and of almost numberless private scholars, to translate the New Testament, the Old Testament, or the whole Bible into clear and readable English: and such efforts have indeed been many, with a goodly number of them possessing real merit. The first official church group effort, responsibly appointed by the major Christian denominations of the British Isles, to ignore the Tyndale-RSV tradition, and to start a new translation-tradition, was by the cooperative committee which is currently at work on the *New English Bible*. The NEB New Testament was published in 1961, with the translators having worked under the direction of the eminent Biblical scholar, C. H. Dodd. Only time will tell what the reaction of the Christian Church in the English-speaking world to this courageous and heroic effort will be. One thing is, however, certain. Just as surely as time brings its changes, including changes in the language we speak, so it will remain the obligation of the church of Christ all through history to see to it that "God's Word Written" is constantly kept available in the living language of the day, so that men and women may ever be in the blessed condition of being made "wise unto salvation" and brought into a living relationship with the saving Christ who is presented in this written Word.

Some Closing Words

We may once more revert to the earnest cry of Judah's King Zedekiah: "Is there any word from the Lord?" And the church of Jesus Christ may joyfully echo the confident assurance of God's faithful spokesman of old, "There is!" We recall also the moving experience of Augustine in the fourth century, who weary of his life of sin one day heard the voice of a child urging again and again, "Take up and read; take up and read!" And when he concluded that the real voice he heard was a divine directive to himself, he did indeed take up the sacred Scriptures, only to be smitten with Holy Spirit conviction when he read there the divine command to renounce the flesh with its lusts and to put on the Lord Jesus. Romans 13:13, 14. And the same God who in the beginning commanded light to shine out of darkness graciously shone into Augustine's dark heart of lust and disobedience and brought to him the illumination of the Holy Spirit, saving faith, and genuine healing of soul and spirit. That same God is still commanding, through the voices of His sons and daughters of the Christian Church, that a lost and weary world shall *take up and read.* These sacred Scriptures, so humble in their literary form, and yet so mighty in their spiritual effectiveness, are still able to cut the human heart with conviction and to awaken faith in the Lord Jesus Christ. Through the distribution of the Scriptures, and through the proclamation of the Word over the pulpit and over the air, all men must hear with their ears the saving Gospel of Jesus Christ! The church cannot afford to forsake the Word to proclaim the word of philosophical speculation nor of scientific or historical research. The church must faithfully proclaim the whole counsel of God so that a world which has lost its way to peace and pardon may through the Word be brought to the "rest" of the people of God.

The church must maintain its awareness of the great source of power which it possesses in the Holy Scriptures. It cannot afford to lose its spiritual effectiveness by preaching any other message than the message of the living Word of God. What a tragedy to lose the heart of the Gospel *kerygma* (proclamation) by turning aside to such peripheral questions as those which belong properly only to advanced scholars: lower and higher criticism, Bible chronology, and the like. And even in schools of higher education scholars must be careful lest they lead the minds and hearts of students away from the central affirmations of the Word to scholarly minutiae which contribute so little to growth in faith, holiness, love, and obedience. It has been well said, for example, that studies in form criticism can become so absorbing and misleading that it is like students of art who become wholly absorbed with such questions as where Raphael got the materials for his paints! (Cf. E. V. Rieu: *The Four Gospels*, Baltimore: Penguin Books [c. 1952], p. xix.)

It is right and proper that the church should, in these days of secularism and liberalism, stress the trustworthy character of the Scriptures. But it must also be emphasized even more that the deepest value of Scripture is to lead us to an encounter with the Saviour, the Lord Jesus Christ. He alone is able to satisfy the spiritual thirst of a hungry soul. As He Himself said,

> If any man thirst,
> let him come unto me,
>> and drink (John 7:37).

And again,

> I am the bread of life:
> he that cometh to me
>> shall never hunger;
> and he that believeth on me
> shall never thirst (John 6:35).

Among the last words of the whole corpus of Scripture is this glorious declaration:

> And the Spirit and the bride say, Come.
> And let him that heareth say, Come.
> And let him that is athirst come.
> And whosoever will,
> let him take the water of life [gratis] Rev. 22:17).

To him whose heart is filled with the words of Holy Writ, there floats also with clear trumpet sound across the millennia from the ancient mountains of Judah the marvelous Gospel call of the prophet of old:

> Ho, every one that thirsteth,
> Come ye to the waters,
> And he that hath no money;
> Come ye, buy, and eat;
> Yea, come, buy wine and milk
>> without money and without price (Isaiah 55:1).

SOLI DEO GLORIA!

[*To God Alone Be the Glory!*]

An Attempt at a Synopsis

Faith in God

Through exposure to the Word of God, with its call to repentance and faith, men of every generation are brought to conversion and the new birth. Such converted people know by immediate awareness that God by His Spirit has sought them out and graciously brought them to new life in Christ. They believe in God, not through a skillful presentation of the theistic proofs, but through the reality of being divinely delivered from the guilt of sin and of experiencing in Christ salvation and healing. The foundation of faith is therefore deeper than logic; it is based on encounter with the living God.

The Word of God

Converted sons and daughters of God have no difficulty then in also believing in divine revelation, for as they hear or read the sacred Scriptures they are aware that they are hearing more than the word of holy men of God; they are listening to the voice of God Himself. Theologians call God's self-disclosure in history divine revelation. Christians accept the Bible as the Word of God not so much because of arguments based on its many excellencies, but because of the inner witness of the Holy Spirit. Such believers, being keenly aware of the God who in Christ has confronted them, find it consonant with their personal experience of God to accept the scriptural reports of how the Word of God came to Moses, Samuel,

Nathan, Isaiah, and Amos. And all through the Old Testament the Word of God (or of Yahweh) refers to the living and powerful word which God gave to His servants, the prophets. In a secondary sense Christ and the apostles can of course also speak of the record of God's self-disclosures as also being the Word of God, for what was originally a spoken Word has in the meantime become an inscripturated or written Word. And just as the proclamation of the message of God to His people through the prophets was called the Word of the Lord, so in the New Testament the proclamation of the saving Gospel of Christ is also called the Word of God or the Word of the Lord.

Full Revelation

But the final and definitive Word of God was neither oral nor inscripturated; it was the personal revelation of God in Jesus Christ. For the WORD became flesh and tabernacled among His people in the first century of this era. The full revelation of God was made only in Christ. And as the Word of the Gospel is proclaimed in every age, men experience afresh a saving encounter with the God of Abraham, Isaac, and Jacob. Their ultimate hope is not merely in a book—marvelous as the characteristics of that Book may be. Their hope is in the One to whom that Book witnesses: the Lord Jesus Christ. He is in very truth the fullness of divine revelation, the express image of the invisible God, the One in whom all the fullness of the Godhead dwelleth bodily. Final authority resides in Him and in Him alone.

Canons of Old and New Testaments

On the authority of Christ Christian believers accept the canonical Scriptures of the Old Testament as God's Word. It is on His assurance, that the Holy Spirit would after Pentecost constitute the apostles as trustworthy interpreters of the Christ event, that Christian believers accept the Scriptures of the New Testament. And because the Holy Spirit remained active in the history of the church of Christ, Christians have no difficulty in believing that the ancient church came to final clarity on the canon of the New Testament

through the work of the Spirit. The essence of the apostolic witness
to Christ may be set down in blank verse:

> GOD
>> who in fragmentary and
>> varied fashion (NEB)
>
> SPAKE
>> in times past unto the fathers
>> by the *prophets*
>
> HATH
>> in these last days
>
> SPOKEN
>> unto us
>> by His *Son* (Heb. 1:1, 2).

With this full blaze of divine revelation in Jesus Christ, how could
anyone return to the less perfect revelation of God in the Old Testament; for ethics, cultus, or theology? And yet we regard ALL of
the Old Testament Scriptures as preparatory for and continuous with
the truths of the New Testament.

The Christ-Witness of Scripture

If men would but use the Scriptures for this divinely intended
purpose of witnessing to Christ and His salvation, there would be
few problems indeed. And in the Anabaptist-Mennonite tradition,
this has been the central emphasis as to the function of the Scriptures. The Bible was viewed as pointing to the Saviour, as calling
men to turn to Him, as the instrument of the Spirit in the birth of
sons and daughters into the family of God. Because Scripture is in
very truth God-given, it is profitable for teaching Christian truth,
for reproving sin, for correcting doctrinal error, for instructing in
divine righteousness. In short, it matures and equips the man of God
to perform good works.

The Limited Purpose of the Scriptures

Intellectual problems arise when men quit using the Scriptures
for their intended soteriological purpose and begin to analyze them

with tools devised for secular books of history and science. And such analysis is surely not to be rejected, for the Scriptures do not lose their power by being studied from every possible angle. There is no merit in taking refuge in ignorance. The Bible is, to be frank, both a divine book, all "God-given," and at the same time it is a genuinely human book: its penmen were genuine authors, each with his own style, viewpoint, and background; they wrote in identifiable human languages; their Semitic thought is everywhere in evidence—vivid, pictorial, concrete. And as an ancient book the Bible shares in the characteristics of the literature of the Ancient New East: a delight in dialogue, no differentiation between direct and indirect quotation, and no critical use of sources. Earthly data is given in the round figures of common people, not with scientific precision (five and twenty or thirty furlongs, two or three firkins, 400 years in Egypt, *pi* is simply three rather than 3.14159265). And the language is generally that of common people, even to the point of using conscious exaggeration: all the cattle of the Egyptians died; all the city was gathered together at the door. People who go to the Bible asking for scientific answers to their questions about the universe are asking the wrong questions of the sacred Scriptures. For these inspired books were not written to tell us the nature of the solar system, nor to anticipate the Linnaean classification of *flora* and *fauna*. Rather, they were written to enlighten us about the salvation which God offers us in Christ. The Scriptures of the Old Covenant witness to this "Son of David" who is to come, and the Scriptures of the New Covenant recite the story of His coming, His life, His cross, and resurrection, and their eternal relevance for our salvation. Although even the history of Christ is not exhaustive, enough has been written to enable us to believe that Jesus is the Messiah predicted in the Old Testament, and by believing on Him to receive life eternal. John 20:31. The Bible is neither a book of science nor an all-comprehensive history. But it is a good and adequate "Map" to glory.

The Holy Spirit and Scripture

The Scriptures may never be viewed as an end in themselves.

Too often have Christians tended in this direction. This tendency to eulogize the Scriptures as if they themselves could save us is actually an ancient Jewish error. Jesus had to rebuke the unbelieving Jews of His day for searching the Scriptures—thinking to find in them eternal life, and failing to realize that the God-intended function of the Scriptures was to witness to the Christ. These blind Bible readers turned away from the One to whom the Scriptures witnessed, and hunted in the sacred scrolls for a salvation which those scrolls could never confer.

Paul teaches the same doctrine. The poor Jews, said he, have a veil over their hearts so that they cannot see the glory of the Son of God as they read the pages of the Old Testament. Only when they turn to the Lord Jesus in repentance and faith will that blinding veil be removed. And this is not only the plight of the Jews. All men outside of Christ, being "natural," are blind to the Deity and Saviourhood of Jesus. They stand in sharp contrast with us who have come to spiritual sight through the blessed ministry of the Spirit. For God who in Genesis 1 commanded the light to shine out of darkness hath shone in our hearts to give the light of the knowledge of the glory of God in the face of Jesus Christ. 2 Cor. 4:6. And so Paul can gratefully refer to us Christians thus: "But we all, with unveiled face, beholding as by reflection [from the pages of Scripture] the glory of the Lord [Jesus], are being changed into the same image from glory to glory, even as by the Lord, the Spirit" (2 Cor. 3:18). Only the Spirit is able to effect this amazing inner transformation.

The Critical Study of Scripture

Students of Holy Scripture may legitimately study every science which throws light on the meaning of the text: archaeology, history, and both literary and form criticism. But at all times there must be the awareness that the critical study of the Bible dare not become a substitute for the Spirit's inner illumination of the penitent and obedient child of God as he feeds on the Word of God for the bread and water of eternal life. Indeed, an overemphasis on technical studies can actually lead to barrenness of soul and coldness of heart.

Once again, this is no plea for a naive attitude, or for ignorance. But it is a reminder that we need to keep in mind what the real nature of the Bible is: God's witness to Christ and His salvation. We cannot afford, therefore, to major in minors, or to become haughty and arrogant "scientific scholars."

The Hermeneutical Community

The Scriptures were intended by God to function as His living oracles in the life of His redeemed Brotherhood. Therefore it is in the assemblies of the saints, where there is freedom to discuss, to differ, to exhort, to teach, to correct one another, that the real truth of His Word gradually comes to light. It is here that genuine binding and loosing take place. It is here that lives are more fully sanctified. It is here that biblical principles are applied to the issues of the day. It is here that the glorified Christ rules and reigns through His Spirit in the hearts and minds of His saints. And it is in such circles that the will of God is discerned, rather than in the "scientific" research of the intellectual world. Just as belief in God is based more on soteriology than on logic, and just as the recognition of His Word comes through the inner witness of the Spirit rather than through arguments based on its excellencies, so the real meaning and significance of the sacred Scriptures is discovered by the sons and daughters of God studying together in the school of Christ, illuminated and guided by His Spirit as free discussion takes place. Linguistic experts are needed, to be sure, and genuine erudition is indeed an asset, but in the final analysis the church of Christ—having met together in the fear of the Lord—must be able to say: "It seemed good to the Holy Spirit and to us. . . ."

A Bibliography for Further Study

Aalders, G. C., *Recent Trends in Old Testament Criticism*. Inter-Varsity, 1938.

Abba, Raymond, *The Nature and Authority of the Bible*. James Clarke, 1958.

Albright, William F., "The Old Testament World," *The Interpreter's Bible*, I, 1952.

_____, *From the Stone Age to Christianity*. Double-day, 1957.

_____, *The Biblical Period*. Biblical Colloquium, 1955.

_____, *The Bible After Twenty Years of Archaeology*. Biblical Colloquium, 1954.

Allis, Oswald T., *God Spake by Moses*. Presbyterian and Reformed, n.d.

_____, *The Five Books of Moses*. Presbyterian and Re-formed, 1943.

Archer, Gleason L., Jr., *A Survey of Old Testament Introduction*. Moody Press, 1964.

Attwater, Donald, Ed., *A Catholic Dictionary*. Macmillan, 1942.

Baillie, John, *The Idea of Revelation in Recent Thought*. Columbia University, 1956.

Balthasar, Hans Urs von, *Word and Revelation: Essays in Theology, I*. Herder and Herder, 1964.

Barth, Karl, *Church Dogmatics*, I/1, T. & T. Clark, 1960; I/2, 1956. A voluminous writer, Barth is a theologian of the Word of God, yet does not demand inerrancy on the part of the Biblical writers. See the Runia volume.

Barth, Markus, *Conversation with the Bible*. Holt, Rinehart and Winston, 1964.

Bartsch, Hans Werner, Ed., *Kerygma and Myth*, by Rudolf Bult-mann *et al*. Harper & Row, 1961.

Bavinck, Herman, *Philosophy of Revelation*. Eerdmans, 1953.

Beegle, Dewey M., *The Inspiration of Scripture*. Westminster, 1963.

Bender, Harold S., *Biblical Revelation and Inspiration*. Herald Press, 1959. An address before Mennonite General Conference by a leading Mennonite scholar, August, 1959.

———————— Ed., *Mennonite Encyclopedia*. Four volumes. Herald Press *et al.*, 1955-59.

Berkhof, Louis, *Principles of Biblical Interpretation*. Baker, 1950.

Berkhouwer, G. C., *General Revelation*. Eerdmans, 1955.

Bewer, Julius A., *The Literature of the Old Testament*. Revised Edition. Columbia University, 1933.

Blackman, E. C., *Biblical Interpretation*. Westminster, 1957.

Boettner, Loraine, *The Inspiration of the Scriptures*. Eerdmans, 1940.

Bouma, Clarence, *et al.*, *The Word of God and the Reformed Faith*. Baker, 1943.

Bouyer, Louis, *The Meaning of Sacred Scripture*. Notre Dame, 1958.

Broderick, Robert C., *Concise Catholic Dictionary*. Bruce, 1944.

Bromiley, G. W., *Karl Barth's Doctrine of Inspiration*. Victoria Institute, 1955.

Broomall, Wick, *Biblical Criticism*. Zondervan, 1957.

Bruce, F. F., *The Apostolic Defence of the Gospel*. Inter-Varsity, 1959.

———————— , *The Christian Approach to the Old Testament*. Inter-Varsity, 1955.

———————— , *The English Bible*, A *History of Translations*. Oxford, 1961.

———————— , *The New Testament Documents: Are They Reliable?* Eerdmans, Fifth Edition, 1960. Bruce is an outstanding evangelical scholar.

———————— , Ed., *Promise and Fulfilment*. T. & T. Clark, 1963.

Brunner, Emil, *Revelation and Reason*. Westminster, 1946. Author of many books of brilliance and learning; highly critical of any doctrine of verbal inspiration. See Jewett's monograph.

Bulst, Werner, S. J., *Revelation*, Sheed and Ward, 1965.

Bultmann, Rudolf, *Theology of the New Testament*, I, II. Scribner, 1951, 1955. See also the volume edited by Bartsch. Bultmann rejects Biblical miracles, even the bodily resurrection of the Lord Jesus, as well as future return in glory.

Burtner, Robert W., and Robert E. Chiles, *A Compend of Wesley's Theology.* Abingdon, 1954.

Buttrick, George A., Ed., *The Interpreter's Dictionary of the Bible.* Four volumes. Abingdon, 1962. Many learned articles, often written from a rather liberal viewpoint.

Carnell, Edward J., *The Case for Orthodox Theology.* Eerdmans, 1959.

Cassels, Louis, *Christian Primer.* Doubleday, 1964.

Cassuto, U., *The Documentary Hypothesis.* Jerusalem: Magnes Press, Hebrew University, 1961. A brilliant and learned defense of the literary unity of the Torah.

Caven, William, "The Testimony of Christ to the Old Testament," *The Fundamentals,* Vol. 4, pp. 46-72.

Charles, R. H., Ed., *The Apocrypha and Pseudepigrapha of the Old Testament,* I, II. Oxford, 1913.

Christian Reformed Church, *Decision of the Synod of 1961 . . . on Infallibility and Inspiration.* Grand Rapids, Michigan.

Clark, Gordon H., *Karl Barth's Theological Method.* Presbyterian and Reformed, 1963.

——————, *Religion, Reason, and Revelation.* Presbyterian and Reformed, 1961. Clark is a staunch believer with an incisive mind.

[Clark, Gordon H., *et al.*], *Can I Trust My Bible?* Moody Press, 1963.

Clarkson, John F., *et al., The Church Teaches.* Herder, 1955.

Craig, Samuel G., *Christianity Rightly So Called.* Presbyterian and Reformed, 1953.

Daniel-Rops, Henri, *What Is the Bible?* Hawthorn. Tenth Printing 1964.

Danielou, Jean, *God and the Ways of Knowing.* World Publishing, 1957.

Davis, John D., Revised by Henry S. Gehman, *The Westminster Dictionary of the Bible.* Westminster, 1944.

Dentan, Robert C., *The Design of the Scriptures.* McGraw-Hill, 1961.

Denzinger, Henry, *The Sources of Catholic Dogma.* Herder, 1957.

DeWolf, L. Harold, *A Theology of the Living Church*. Harper, 1953.
Dillenberger, John, "On Broadening the New Hermeneutic," *The New Hermeneutic*. Harper & Row, 1964.
Dodd, C. H., *The Authority of the Bible*. Harper, 1962.
——————, *The Bible To-Day*. Cambridge: Macmillan, 1947.
Dods, Marcus, *The Bible, Its Origin and Nature*. Scribner, 1921.
Douglas, J. D., Ed., *The New Bible Dictionary*. Eerdmans, 1962.
Ebeling, Gerhard, "The Significance of the Critical Historical Method . . .," *Word and Faith*. Fortress, 1962.
——————, "Word of God and Hermeneutic," *The New Hermeneutic*. Harper & Row, 1964.
——————, *Word and Faith*. Fortress, 1963.
Ellis, E. Earle, *Paul's Use of the Old Testament*. Eerdmans, 1957.
Engelder, Theodore, *Scripture Cannot Be Broken*. Concordia, 1944.
Evangelical Theological Society:
   Papers Read at the Annual Meetings (Mimeographed).
   The Quarterly *Bulletin*, 1958-.
Farrar, Frederic W., *History of Interpretation*. Baker, 1961.
Filson, Floyd V., *Which Books Belong in the Bible?* Westminster, 1957.
Fitchett, W. H., *Where the Higher Criticism Fails*. Epworth, 1922.
Forsyth, T. P., *The Principle of Authority*. Hodder & Stoughton, n.d.
Friberg, H. Daniel, "The Bible and Propositional Truth," *Christianity Today* (VII, 20, July 5, 1963), pp. 975-77.
Fuchs, Ernst, "The New Testament and the Hermeneutical Problem," *The New Hermeneutic*. Harper & Row, 1964.
Funk, Robert W., "The Hermeneutical Problem and Historical Criticism," *The New Hermeneutic*. Harper & Row, 1964.
Fundamentals, The. Twelve volumes. Chicago: Testimony Publishing Company, c. 1909-c. 1915.
Gaebelein, Frank E., *The Meaning of Inspiration*. Inter-Varsity, 1950.
——————, *The Pattern of God's Truth*. Oxford, 1954.
Gaussen, L., *Theopneustia, The Plenary Inspiration of the Holy Scriptures*. Institute Colportage Association, n.d.

Geldenhuys, J. Norval, *Supreme Authority*. Eerdmans, 1953.

Gerstner, John H., "The Nature of Revelation," *Christian Faith and Modern Theology*. Channel Press, 1964.

Grant, Robert M., *The Bible in the Church, A Short History of Interpretation*. Macmillan, 1960.

Gray, James M., "The Inspiration of the Bible," *The Fundamentals*, Vol. 3, pp. 7-41.

Greenlee, J. Harold, *Introduction to New Testament Textual Criticism*. Eerdmans, 1964.

Guillebaud, H. E., *Some Moral Difficulties of the Bible*. Inter-Varsity, 1941.

Hackett, Stuart C., *The Resurrection of Theism*. Moody Press, 1957.

Hadjiantoniou, George A., *New Testament Introduction*. Moody Press, 1957.

Hahn, Herbert F., *Old Testament in Modern Research*. Muhlenberg Press, 1954.

Harkness, Georgia, *Foundations of Christian Knowledge*. Abingdon, 1955.

Harris, R. Laird, *Inspiration and Canonicity of the Bible*. Zondervan, 1957.

Harrison, Everett F., "Criteria of Biblical Inerrancy," *Christianity Today* (II, 8, Jan. 20, 1958), pp. 16-18.

_____ , *Introduction to the New Testament*. Eerdmans, 1964.

Hebert, A. G., *The Authority of the Old Testament*. Faber & Faber, 1947.

Hebert, Gabriel, *Fundamentalism and the Church.* Westminster, 1957.

Henry, Carl F. H., *Evangelical Responsibility in Contemporary Theology*. Eerdmans.

Henry, Carl F. H., Ed., *Christian Faith and Modern Theology*. Channel Press, 1964.

_____ , *Contemporary Evangelical Thought*. Channel Press, 1957.

_____ , *Basic Christian Doctrines*. Holt, Rinehart and Winston, 1962.

_____ , *Revelation and the Bible*. Baker, 1958.

Hills, Edward F. *The King James Version Defended!* Christian Research Press, 1956.

Hodgson, Leonard, *et al.*, *On the Authority of the Bible.* London: S. P. C. K., 1960.

Hofmann, Johann C. K. von, *Interpreting the Bible.* Augsburg, 1959.

Horsch, John, *Mennonites in Europe.* Mennonite Publishing House, 1950.

Hunter, Archibald M., *Interpreting the New Testament, 1900-1950.* Westminster, n.d.

————————, *Introducing New Testament Theology.* Westminster, n.d.

Huxtable, John, *The Bible Says.* John Knox, 1962.

Hyatt, J. Philip, *The Heritage of Biblical Faith.* Bethany Press, 1964.

Illingworth, J. R., *Reason and Revelation.* Macmillan, 1903.

Jewett, Paul King, *Emil Brunner's Concept of Revelation.* James Clarke, 1954.

Johnson, Douglas, *The Christian and His Bible.* Eerdmans, 1960.

Johnson, Robert Clyde, *Authority in Protestant Theology.* Westminster, 1959.

Jones, D. Martyn Lloyd, *Authority.* Inter-Varsity, 1957.

Jones, H. Cunliffe, *The Authority of the Biblical Revelation.* Pilgrim Press, 1948.

Kantzer, Kenneth S., "Inspiration," *Zondervan Pictorial Bible Dictionary.* 1963.

Keene, J. Calvin, *et al.*, *The Western Heritage of Faith and Reason.* Harper & Row, 1963.

Kelly, Balmer H., Ed., *Introduction to the Bible. The Layman's Bible Commentary.* John Knox, 1959.

Kelly, Howard A., *A Scientific Man and the Bible.* Harper, 1925.

Kenyon, Frederic G., *Our Bible and the Ancient Manuscripts.* Harper. Fifth Edition, 1958.

Kerr, Hugh T., *A Compend of Luther's Theology.* Westminster, 1943.

Klassen, William, and Graydon Snyder, Eds., *Current Issues in New Testament Interpretation.* Harper & Row, 1962.

Kraeling, Emil G., *The Old Testament Since the Reformation.* Harper, 1955.

Kraus, C. Norman, Ed., *Evangelicalism and Anabaptism*. Herald Press, 1979.

Lindsay, Thomas M., "The Doctrine of Scripture: The Reformers and the Princeton School," *The Expositor* (London, Fifth Series, Vol. 1, 1895), pp. 278-93.

Margalioth, Rachel, *The Indivisible Isaiah*. Yeshiva University, 1964.

Martin, Hugh, and R. Bremner, *Inspiration of Scripture*. Inverness: Free Presbyterian Church of Scotland Publications Committee, 1964.

McKenzie, John L., *The Two-Edged Sword*. Bruce, 1956.

Menno Simons, Complete Writings of. Verduin-Wenger edition. Herald Press, 1956.

Mennonite Church, General Conference, *A Christian Declaration on the Authority of the Scriptures*. Newton, Kansas, 1962.

Mennonite Church, General Conference, *Minutes, Study Commission on Inspiration of the Scriptures*. Newton, Kansas, January 27, 28, 1961 (Mimeographed).

Mennonite Confession of Faith. Herald Press, 1963.

"Mennonite General Conference on Biblical Inspiration," *Gospel Herald* (LII, 37, Sept. 22, 1959), p. 785.

Metzger, Bruce Manning, *The Text of the New Testament, Its Transmission, Corruption, and Restoration*. Oxford, 1964. The classic in its field.

Mickelsen, A. Berkeley, *Interpreting the Bible*. Eerdmans, 1963. Review by John Murray, *Westminster Theological Journal* (XXVI, 1, Nov. 1964), pp. 31-33.

Miller, Donald G., *Neglected Emphases in Biblical Criticism*. Union Theological Seminary, Richmond, 1945.

Miller, H. S., *General Biblical Introduction*. Word-Bearer Press. Fourth Edition, 1947. Contains a remarkable amount of information.

Möller, Wilhelm, *Grundriss fur Alttestamentliche Einleitung*. Berlin: Evangelische Verlagsanstalt, 1958. A conservative and scholarly monograph.

Murray, John, *Calvin on Scripture and Divine Sovereignty*. Baker.

1960.

Nash, Ronald H., *The New Evangelicalism*. Zondervan, 1963.

Neill, Stephen, *The Interpretation of the New Testament, 1861-1961*. Oxford, 1964.

Niebuhr, H. Richard, *The Meaning of Revelation*, Macmillan. Seventh Printing, 1960.

Nineham, D. E., Ed., *The Church's Use of the Bible*. S. P. C. K., 1963.

Nygren, Anders, *The Significance of the Bible for the Church*. Fortress, 1963.

Orr, James, "The Early Narratives of Genesis," *The Fundamentals*, Vol. 6, pp. 85-97.

——————————, "Holy Scripture and Modern Negations," *The Fundamentals*, Vol. 9, pp. 31-47.

——————————, *Revelation and Inspiration*. Scribner, 1910; Eerdmans, 1952.

Packer, J. I., *"Fundamentalism" and the Word of God*. Eerdmans, 1958.

——————————, *God Speaks to Man. Revelation and the Bible*. Westminster, 1966.

Parente, Pietro, *et al.*, *Dictionary of Dogmatic Theology*. Bruce, 1951.

Patton, Francis L., *Fundamental Christianity*. Macmillan, 1928.

Payne, J. Barton, *The Theology of the Older Testament*. Zondervan, 1962.

Pfeiffer, Robert H., *Introduction to the Old Testament*. Revised Edition, Harper, 1948.

Preus, Robert, "Current Theological Problems Which Confront Our Church" (Mimeographed).

——————————, *The Inspiration of Scripture*. Oliver & Boyd, 1955.

——————————, "Notes on the Inerrancy of Scripture" (Mimeographed).

Rahner, Karl, *Inspiration in the Bible*. Herder & Herder. Fourth Impression, 1963. (Original German Title, *Über die Schriftinspiration.*)

Ramm, Bernard, *The Pattern of Authority*. Eerdmans, 1957.

_____, *Protestant Biblical Interpretation*. Wilde, 1956.

_____, *Special Revelation and the Word of God*. Eerdmans, 1961.

_____, *The Witness of the Spirit*. Eerdmans, 1960.

Reformed Ecumenical Synod of 1958: *Report of the Committee on the Inspiration of Scripture* (Mimeographed). *Acts of the Fourth Reformed Ecumenical Synod of Potchefstroom, South Africa, August 6-13, 1958, pp. 33-56*.

Reid, J. K. S., *The Authority of Scripture*. Methuen. 1957.

Reu, John Michael, *Luther and the Scriptures*. Wartburg, 1944.

Richardson, Alan, *Christian Apologetics*. SCM, 1947.

_____, *Preface to Bible Study*. SCM, Eighth Edition, 1956.

_____, Ed., *A Theological Word Book of the Bible*. Macmillan, 1960.

_____ and W. Schweitzer, Eds., *Biblical Authority for Today*. Westminster, SCM, 1951.

Ridderbos, H. N., *The Authority of the New Testament Scriptures*. Presbyterian and Reformed, 1963.

Ridderbos, H. N., *When the Time Had Fully Come*. Eerdmans, 1957.

Ridderbos, N. H., *Is There a Conflict Between Genesis 1 and Natural Science?* Eerdmans, 1957.

Roberts, Bleddyn J., *The Old Testament Texts and Versions*. University of Wales, 1951. An excellent monograph.

Robertson, E. H., *The Bible in Our Time, The Recovery of Confidence*. Association Press, 1961.

Robinson, H. Wheeler, *Inspiration and Revelation in the Old Testament*. Oxford. Fifth Impression, 1960.

Robinson, James M., "Hermeneutics Since Barth," *The New Hermeneutic*. Harper & Row, 1964.

_____ and John B. Cobb, Jr., *New Frontiers in Theology*, Vol. II, *The New Hermeneutic*. Harper & Row, 1964. Note William E. Hull's discerning review of this work in *Review and Expositor* (LXII, 2, Spring 1965), pp. 227-29.

Rowley, H. H., *The Unity of the Bible*. Westminster, n.d. [1953]

Rowley has written many monographs on the Bible, especially on the Old Testament.

Runia, Klaas, *Karl Barth's Doctrine of Scripture*. Eerdmans, 1962.

Rust, Eric C., *Salvation History*. John Knox, 1962.

Ryrie, Charles C., *Neo-Orthodoxy*. Moody Press, 1956.

Sasse, Hermann, "A Binding Dogma: The Inspiration of Holy Scripture," *Christianity Today* (VI, 12, March 16, 1962), pp. 563-65.

Smart, James D., *The Interpretation of Scripture*. Westminster, 1961.

Smith, Wilbur M., *Therefore Stand*. Wilde, 1945.

Snaith, Norman H., *The Inspiration and Authority of the Bible*. Epworth, 1958.

Stevick, Daniel B., *Beyond Fundamentalism*. John Knox, 1964.

Stonehouse, N. B., and Paul Woolley, Eds., *The Infallible Word*. Eerdmans, 1953. A series of excellent essays on the Bible by faculty members from Westminster Theological Seminary, Philadelphia.

Tenney, Merrill C., Ed., *The Word for This Century*. Oxford, 1960.

——————— , *The Zondervan Pictorial Bible Dictionary*. 1963.

Terry, Milton S., *Biblical Hermeneutics*. Zondervan, n.d.

Thiele, Edwin R., *The Mysterious Numbers of the Hebrew Kings*. University of Chicago, 1955. A real contribution to understanding Old Testament chronology.

Thomas, John Newton, "How Barth Has Influenced Me," *Theology Today* (XIII, 3, Oct. 1956), pp. 368, 369. Many other responses to Barth in this issue.

Thompson, J. A., *Archaeology and the New Testament*. Eerdmans, 1960.

——————— , *Archaeology and the Old Testament*. Eerdmans, 1957.

Todd, John M., Ed., *Problems of Authority*. Helicon, 1962.

Twilley, L. D., *The Origin and Transmission of the New Testament*. Eerdmans, 1957.

Unger, Merrill F., *Unger's Bible Dictionary*. Moody Press, 1957.

Van Til, Cornelius, *The New Modernism*. Presbyterian and Reformed, 1947.

——————— , *Christianity and Barthianism*. Presbyterian and

Reformed, 1962.

Vine, W. E., *The Divine Inspiration of the Bible*. Pickering & Inglis, n.d. [1923]

Vischer, Wilhelm, *The Witness of the Old Testament to Christ*. Lutterworth, 1949.

Vos, Johannes G., "Bible," *Encyclopedia of Christianity*, I. National Foundation for Christian Education, 1964.

Walvoord, John F., Ed., *Inspiration and Interpretation*. Eerdmans, 1957.

Warfield, B. B., *Revelation and Inspiration*. Oxford, 1927. Largely reprinted as *The Inspiration and Authority of the Bible*. Presbyterian and Reformed, 1948. Warfield is the classic defender of the "high view" of the Bible.

Westermann, Claus, Ed., *Essays on Old Testament Hermeneutics*. John Knox, 1963.

Wilder, Amos N., "New Testament Hermeneutics Today," *Current Issues in New Testament Interpretation*. Harper & Row, 1962.
_____ , "The Word as Address and the Word as Meaning," *The New Hermeneutic*. Harper & Row, 1964.

Wilson, Robert Dick, *A Scientific Investigation of the Old Testament*. Moody Press, 1959.
_____ , *Studies in the Book of Daniel*. First Series, Putnam, 1917. Second Series, edited by O. T. Allis, Revell, 1938.

Wood, James D., *The Interpretation of the Bible*. Duckworth, 1958.

Wright, G. Ernest, *God Who Acts*. Fifth Impression. SCM, 1960.
_____ , *Biblical Archaeology*. Westminster: Duckworth, 1957.
John Bright pronounces this book, "The best survey of the subject."

Young, Edward J., *An Introduction to the Old Testament*. Eerdmans. 1949.
_____ , *Thy Word Is Truth*. Eerdmans, 1957.
_____ , *Who Wrote Isaiah?* Eerdmans, 1958.

Many treatises on systematic theology have fairly thorough treatments of the doctrine of Scripture. And Bible dictionaries have articles on every topic involved in the studies of this book.

INDEX

A

Aalders, G. C., 145
Aaron, 16, 90
Abba, Raymond, 145
Abraham, 37, 40, 71, 87, 90, 91, 99
Abram, 16
Acts, Book of, 19, 37, 74, 80, 82, 83, 97, 101-104, 124
Acts of God (See God who acts)
Adam, 14
Aelfric, 124
Aesthetic stimulation, 37
Agape love, 59, 75, 80
Age of the earth, 34
Albright, William F., 30, 31, 110, 145
Aldhelm, 124
Aldred, 124
Alexander, Cecil F., 84
Alexandrian text, 113, 116
Alfred, King, 124
Allegorical interpretation, 56
Allegory, 36, 37, 62
Allis, Oswald T., 7, 145
American Standard Version, 108, 119, 121, 133
Amos, 17, 26, 81, 104
Anabaptists and Anabaptism, 7, 59, 60, 68, 80
Anagogical interpretation, 57
Ancient books, 33
Andrewes, Dean, 130
Anglican Church and Anglicans, 60, 129-131
Annas, 73
"Anointed," 96
Anonymous books, 28
Anthropology of the Bible, 86, 87
Antioch in Pisidia, 103
Antioch in Syria, 112
Antwerp, 127
Apocalypse (See Revelation of John)
Apocrypha, O. T., 127, 129, 130, 134
Apostles, 74, 98
Apostolicity, 58, 77
Aqiba, Rabbi, 110
Aramaic, 32, 50, 61
Archer, Gleason L., Jr., 27, 43, 145
Ark (of the testimony), 18
Arles, 123
Armenian Version, 114
Arminianism, 83
Arundel, Archbishop, 125

Ascension of Christ, 104, 123
Asherah, 66, 67
Associated Mennonite Biblical Seminaries, 3, 8
Assyria, 15, 35
Astronomy, 34
Athanasius, 77
Atonement of Christ, 41
Attwater, Donald, 77, 145
Augsburger, Myron S., 8
Augustine, Aurelius, 55, 78, 121, 136
Augustine of Canterbury, 123
Aurochs, 66
Austria, 59
Authority of Scripture, 32-54, especially 42
Authorship and date, 27
Avenger of blood, 75

B

Baal, 67, 108
Baber, Henry, 125
Babylon, 15, 26, 35, 65, 67
Bagster, Hexapla, 125
Baillie, John, 13, 52, 145
Balthasar, H. U. von, 145
Bancroft, Richard, 130
Baptism, 59, 60, 80-82
Baptism with the Spirit, 82
Baptists, 132
Barker, Robert, 131
Barr, James, 8
Barth, Karl, 7, 30, 31, 41, 42, 55, 145
Barth, Markus, 145
Bartsch, H. W., 145
Basin and towel, 81, 82
Bats and birds, 42, 43
Baur, 24
Bavinck, Herman, 145
Bede, 124
Beegle, Dewey M., 145
ben Asher, Aaron, 110
ben Chayim, Jacob, 110
ben Naphtali, 110
Bender, Harold S., 7, 8, 135, 146
Berkhof, Louis, 56, 77, 146
Berkhouwer, G. C., 146
Bethlehem, 73, 96
Bewer, J. A., 28, 109, 146
Bible reading, Lifelong, 84
Biblical authority, 42
Biblical history, 61
Biblical introduction, 61
Biblical theology, 30, 61
Bilson, Thomas, 131
Biology, 34
Birth of Christ, 39

Bishops' Bible, 130
Blackman, E. C., 146
Blanke, Fritz, 7
Blayney, Benjamin, 131
"Blindness" in reading Scripture, 104
Blindness of the unregenerated, 54
Blood of Christ, 68, 71, 74, 85, 98
Bloody Mary, 128
Boettner, Loraine, 146
Bones of paschal lamb not broken, 101
Book of Jashar, 51
Book of the Acts of Solomon, 51
Book of the Chronicles, 51
Book of the Kings, 51
Book of the Law of Moses, 49
Book of the Wars of the Lord, 51
Bosheth, 108
Bouma, Clarence, 146
Bouyer, Louis, 146
"Branch," 94, 100
Bremner, R., 151
Brethren in Christ, 80
Britain, Great, 121
Britons, 121, 122
Broderick, R. C., 146
Broken, Scripture cannot be, 22, 32
Bromiley, G. W., 146
Broomall, Wick, 146
Brotherly instruction, 56
Browne, Bishop, 132
Bruce, F. F., 8, 125, 146
Brunner, Emil, 7, 55, 146
Bulst, Werner, 146
Bultmann, Rudolf, 146
Burtner, R. W., 147
Buttrick, George A., 147
Byzantine text, 112-114, 116
Byzantium, 112, 113

C

Caedman, 123
Caesarea Philippi, 97
Caesarean text, 113
Caiaphas, 73
Calvin, John, 44, 55, 56, 59, 129
Cambridge University, 126, 130
Canaan, 14-16, 24, 65, 87, 90
Canaanites, 49, 67
Canons of Scripture, 23, 37, 50, 77
Canterbury revision, 132
Capernaum, 100
Capital punishment, 59, 75
Carlson, Anton, 8
Carnell, Edward J., 147
Cassels, Louis, 147
Cassuto, Umberto, 29, 48, 147

Caven, William, 147
Celibate clergy, 59
Celtic Saxon, 123
Celts, 121
Ceremonial law, 59, 71
Charles, R. H., 50, 147
Chaucer, 122
Christ and Scripture, 50, 51, 71
Christ as Judge, 102
Christ as Lord, 105
Christ as Mediator of a New Covenant, 69
Christ as Redeemer, 14, 15
Christ as unifying theme of Scripture, 42,
  73, 86-105
Christ as Word of God, 20, 21, 32, 57, 98
Christ born, 15, 39
Christ (See also ascension, resurrection)
Christian Reformed Church, Decisions of,
  147
Christocentric Bible, 58, 59, 70, 72-74,
  86-105
Christological interpretation, 72-74
Christ's doctrine of Scripture normative,
  8, 48, 74
Chronicles, 51, 107-109
Chronicles of Gad, 51
Chronicles of Iddo, 51
Chronicles of Jehu, 51
Chronicles of Nathan, 51
Chronicles of Samuel, 51
Chronicles of Shemaiah, 51
Chronicles of the Seers, 51
Chronology of the Bible, 137
Church, 42, 52, 55, 58, 59, 67, 71, 84, 98
Church and state, 69
Church of the Brethren, 80
Circumcision, 71, 79
Clark, Gordon H., 147
Clarkson, John F., 147
Clement, 113
Clement VII, 126
Cleopas, 104
Cobb, John B., 56
Codices, New Testament, 113
Cognate languages, 47
Cologne, 126
Colossians, 71
Combining of Biblical books, 28
Commentary on the Book of Kings, 51
Coney (rock badger), 43
Conflate readings, 120
Congregationalists, 132
Conscience, Liberty of, 160
Conscious exaggeration, 33
Consensus of scholarship, 30
Constance, Council of, 126

Constantine, 116
Constantinople, 112, 113
Context, 58, 65
Corinthians, 53, 56, 71, 74, 80, 82, 105
Corpus Christi College, 130
Covenant, 133
Covenant with Abraham, 14, 71, 89, 99
Covenant with Israel, 15, 40, 88, 89
Covenant with Noah, 14
Covenants, Old vs. New, 60
Coverdale, Miles, 127-129
Craig, Samuel G., 147
Cranmer, Thomas, 127-129
Creation, 14, 34-37, 40, 71, 88
Creeds of the church, 84
Crete, 65
Critical questions, 29
Cromwell, Thomas, 128
Crucifixion of Christ, 40, 101
Cud, Chewing of the, 43
Cursive manuscripts, 118
Cyprian, 113

D

Dan, 49
Daniel, 18, 25, 37, 96, 97, 123
Danielou, Jean, 147
Daniel-Rops, Henri, 147
Date, Questions of, 27
David, 16, 18, 24, 80, 92-94, 101, 103
Davis, John D., 147
Day, George E., 133
"Days" of creation, 78
Dead Sea scrolls, 51, 106, 109
Death and mortality, 38
Death penalty, 59
Deity of the Messiah, 93, 96
Demons, 133
Dentan, Robert C., 147
Denzinger, Henry, 147
Depravity, 36, 86, 87
Deus absconditus, 21
Deus revelatus, 21
Deuteronomy, 48, 49, 75, 76, 92, 102, 107
Developments in Biblical scholarship, 30
DeWolf, L. Harold, 148
Dictation theories, 44
Dillenberger, John, 148
Diognetus, Epistle to, 111
Diphath, 107
Discrepancies, Apparent, 44
Distortion of Biblical truth, 80
Dividing of Biblical books, 28
Dividing of Hebrew words, 108
Divination, 121

Divine and human elements in Scripture, 41
Divine image, 14, 35
Divorce and remarriage, 75, 76
Documentary hypothesis, 29, 48
Dodd, C. H., 135, 148
Dods, Marcus, 148
Douglas, J. D., 148
Dreams, 25
Druid religion, 121
Dynamical inspiration, 52

E

Earth, Age of, 34
Eastern Mennonite College, 7, 8
Ebeling, Gerhard, 148
Ecclesiastes, 37-39
Eclecticism in textual criticism, 117
Eden, Garden of, 14
Editing of Hebrew manuscripts, 49, 50
Edom, 107
Egypt and Egyptians, 33, 65, 67, 87, 90, 98, 100
Eichrodt, Walter, 7
Einstein, 43
Eli, House of, 17
Eliphaz, 64
Elizabeth, Queen, 129
Elizabethan English, 133, 134
Ellicott, C. J., 132
Ellis, E. Earle, 148
Emendation of Hebrew text, 108
Emmaus, 104
Emptiness of the "natural" life, 38
Engelder, Theodore, 148
England Christianized, 123
English Bibles, 123-136
English language, 121, 122
English Revised Version, 132, 133
Engrafted Word, 18
Enss, Gustav H., 7
Enuma elish, 35
Ephesians, 83, 126
Erasmus, 57, 114, 115, 126
Erb, Paul, 8
Error in Scripture, Charge of, 41
Esau's wives, 39
Eshbaal, 108
Essex, 122
Ethiopian, 74
Etymology, Limitations of, 46, 47, 62
Euphemisms, 63
Eusebius, 114
Evangelical Theological Society, 148
Evangelicals and Evangelicalism, 24, 30, 47

Evolution of religion, 28, 31
Exaggeration, 63
Exodus, Book of, 33, 49, 65, 75, 123
Exodus of Israel from Egypt, 15, 39, 40, 71, 90, 103
Ex opere operato, 81
Ezekiel, 16, 17, 65
Ezra, Book of, 106, 109
Ezra, the Scribe, 49, 50

F

Faith essential in interpreter, 57
Faith vs. pessimism, 37
Faith, Voice of, 38
"Faithful and True," 21
Fall, Account of the, 37
Fallible, The church, 42
Family, 113, 118
Farrar, F. W., 56, 148
Fasts, 59
Figurative language, 73
Figures of speech, 62-65
File (tool), 66
Filson, Floyd V., 148
Fitchett, W. H., 148
"Flesh" evil, 87
Flora and fauna, 34
Focus, Biblical truth in, 79-85
Foot washing, 80, 82
Form criticism, 137
Former prophets, 16
Fornication, 76
Forsyth, T. P., 148
Fourth Ezra, 50
Freedom of conscience, 60
Friberg, H. Daniel, 148
Frisian language, 122
Froben, Johann, 114
Fuchs, Ernst, 148
Fundamentals, The, 14, 148
Funk, Robert W., 148

G

Gabriel, 99
Gaebelein, Frank E., 148
Galatians, 23, 56, 71, 91
Galaxies, 34
Galilee, 100
Gaussen, L., 148
Geldenhuys, J. Norval, 148
General revelation, 70
Genesis, 14, 23, 35, 36, 42, 44, 48, 49, 76, 86, 90-92, 123
Geneva, 129
Geneva Bible, 129, 130
Gentiles, 74, 84, 95, 99

Geocentric account, 34
Geology, 34
Georgian Version, 114
German-English similarities, 122, 123
Germany, 59, 126
Gerstner, John H., 149
Glosses in text, 118
God who acts, 14, 25, 40, 57, 88, 90, 97
Gog and Magog, 65
Golgotha, 91, 98
Goshen College, 3, 7
Goshen College Biblical Seminary, 8, 9
Gospel of Christ, 18-20
Gospels, 37, 40, 124
Grace of God, 71, 79, 81-83, 98
Graf-Wellhausen hypothesis, 48, 49
Grammatical interpretation, 61-64
Grant, Robert M., 56, 149
Gray, James M., 149
Graybill, John B., 66
Grebel, Conrad, 59
Grebel Lectures, 5
Greek, 32, 57, 126, 131, 132
Greek New Testament, 111-121
Green, William Henry, 133
Greenlee, J. H., 121, 149
Gregory, C. R., 117
Gregory, Pope, 123
Gressman, Hugo, 48
Griesbach, J. J., 115
"Groves" (Asherah), 66, 67
Guillebaud, H. E., 149
Gut, Walter, 7

H

Habakkuk, 26, 37
Hackett, Stuart C., 149
Hades, 20
Hadjiantoniou, G. A., 149
Hahn, Herbert F., 149
Hail, Plague of, 33
Hampton Court, 130
Harding, John, 130
Harkness, Georgia, 149
Harper Study Bible, 29
Harris, R. Laird, 149
Harrison, E. F., 41, 149
Heaven, 123
Hebert, A. G., 149
Hebert, Gabriel, 149
Hebrew Old Testament, 106-111, 126
Hebrew tongue, 32, 57, 61, 126
Hebrews, 19, 24, 27, 32, 37, 44, 56, 68, 71, 74, 79, 98
Hell, 123

Helps in Bible study, 61
Henry, Carl F. H., 149
Henry VIII, King, 127, 128
Henry, Matthew, 43
Hereford, N. de, 124
Hermeneutics, 55-85
Herod, 102
Herod the Great, 96
Hershberger, Guy F., 8
Hexateuch, 47
Hieroglyphics, 65
Higher criticism, 9, 28-30, 137
Hillel, Codex, 110
Hills, Edward F., 149
Historical criticism, 41
Historical interpretation, 64
Historical research, 77
History, God and, 36, 90
History in the Bible, 37, 39, 40 (See also, God who acts)
History of Nathan, 51
Hodge, A. A., 52
Hodgson, Leonard, 150
Hofmann, J. C. K. von, 56, 150
"Holding out," 83
Holiness of Christians, 82
Holy kiss, 81
Holy Spirit, 15, 23, 31, 32, 36, 41, 42, 52, 55, 79, 91, 98-100, 104, 136
Holy Spirit and Scripture, 53, 54, 57, 76, 82, 83, 102, 103, 120
Holy Spirit conception, 98
"Hornet," 65
Horsch, John, 69, 150
Horst, I. B., 8
Hort, F. J. A. (See Westcott and Hort), 113
Hosea, 17, 100
Housman, A. E., 117, 120
Human, The Bible, 33, 42
Hunter, A. M., 150
Huxtable, John, 150
Hyatt, J. Philip, 150

I

Idealism vs. Christian faith, 40
Idolatry, 15
Illingworth, J. R., 150
Illumination, 78, 84
Illustrative use of O.T., 45
Image, Divine, 14, 35
Immanuel, 96, 98
Imminence of Christ's return, 78
Incarnation of Christ, 20, 74
Inerrancy of Scripture, 41
Infallibility, Non-, of church, 42
Infallibility of Scripture, 51

Infant baptism, 59, 60, 69
Inscripturation of the Word, 22, 58
Inspiration, How name? 51-53
Inspiration of Scripture, 32-54
International Council of Religious Education, 134
Interpretation in the N.T., 44
Interpretation of Christ's life and death, 100
Interpretation of God's acts, 26
Interpretation of Scripture, 55-85
Interpretation, Prophetic, of God's acts, 26
Iota, 51
Ireland, 123
Irenaeus, 113
Iron, 66
Isaac, 37, 89, 90
Isaiah, 16, 17, 23, 26, 28, 29, 63-65, 73, 81, 99, 101, 109
Ishtar, 67
Israel (Jacob), 87
Israel (people and nation), 15, 17, 35, 37, 47, 67, 68, 70, 74, 88, 89, 92, 93, 98, 99
"It stands written," 31
Italic type, 129

J

Jacob, 37, 44, 90, 92, 98
Jahweh, 16 and passim
James, 18, 37
James, Epistle of, 104
James I, King, 129, 130
James, Fleming, 134
Jehovah, 134
Jeremiah, 16-18, 27, 44, 55, 67, 68, 86, 93, 109
Jerome, 111
Jerubbaal, 108
Jerubbesheth, 108
Jerusalem, 65, 104
Jesus Christ, 20-23, 32, 98 and passim
Jewett, Paul King, 150
Jewish canon, 77
Jewish hermeneutics, 56
Joel, 17, 101
John, 19, 20, 30, 34, 55, 74, 80, 82, 84, 96, 100, 101
John the Baptist, 73, 97, 99
Johnson, Douglas, 150
Johnson, Robert Clyde, 150
Jonah, 39
Jonathan, 109
Jones, D. Martyn Lloyd, 150
Jones, H. Cunliffe, 150
Jordan, 73

Joseph, 89, 90, 98
Joshua (book), 16, 28, 51, 65, 75, 109
Judah (man), 92
Judah (tribe or people), 15, 17, 26, 65, 67, 93
Judas, 101
Jude, 37, 83
Judges, Book of, 16, 28, 37, 39, 75, 109
Judges called Elohim, 22
Justification by faith, 58
Jutes, 122

K

Kahle, Paul, 110
Kantzer, Kenneth S., 44, 150
Kauffman, Nelson E., 8
Keene, J. Calvin, 150
Kelly, Balmer H., 150
Kelly, Howard A., 150
Kent, 122, 123
Kenyon, Frederick, 121, 150
Keraia, 51
Kerr, Hugh T., 150
Kerygma, 40, 72, 73, 102, 137
Kilpatrick Greek New Testament, 116
King James Version, 108, 115, 118, 120, 121, 127, 129-134
"King of kings," 21, 105
Kings, Book of, 17, 28, 51, 109
Kittel Hebrew Bible, 110, 111
Klassen, William, 150
Knox, John, 129
Köberle, Adolf, 7
Köhler, Ludwig, 7
Koine Greek, 32, 61
Kraeling, Emil G., 150
Kuiper, R. B., 7
Kümmel, Werner G., 7

L

Laish, 49
Language of Genesis 1, 34, 35
Latimer, 129
Latourette, Kenneth Scott, 123
Latter prophets, 17
Law of Moses, 27
Lectionary manuscripts, 111, 112
Legends, 26, 36, 50
Lehman, Chester K., 7, 8, 135
Leningrad Ms. ("L"), 110
Levites, 18
Leviticus, 43, 75, 108
Lewis, John, 125
Lind, Millard C., 135
Lindsay, Thomas M., 151
Lindsell, Harold, 29, 49

Linnaeus, 43
Literal interpretation, 57
Literary criticism, 47-50
Literary variety, 37
Litigation, 75
"Living soul," 35
Lord's Supper, 80, 81
Lots, at Christ's cross, 101
Lower criticism, 137
Lucian of Antioch, 112
Luke, 19, 72, 73, 78, 83, 99, 104
Luther Bible, 57
Luther, Martin, 45, 55-59, 122, 127

M

Maccabees, 97
Machen, J. Gresham, 7
McKenzie, John L., 151
MacRae, Allan A., 7
Madden, Fr., 125
Magistracy, 59
Maimonides, 110
Manna, 90
Manz, Felix, 59
"Map," Scripture as a, 45, 46
Marduk, 35
Margalioth, Rachel, 29, 151
Mark, 77
Marpeck, Pilgram, 59
Marriage, Christ on, 76
Martin, Hugh, 150
Mary, Queen, 128, 129
Masoretes, 106
Masoretic Hebrew text, 50, 106, 108, 109
Mass, 59
Matthew, 51, 73, 76, 80, 82, 83, 99, 100
Matthew's Bible, 128
Meaning of God's acts, 26, 40
Meaning of Scripture, 55-85
Menno Simons, 151
Mennonite Confession of Faith, 70, 151
Mennonite Encyclopedia, 70
Mennonite General Conference, 70, 151
Mennonites, 69, 80, 135
Meritorious works, 59
Messianic prophecy, 72, 73, 90-105
Metaphor, 62
Methodists, 132
Metonymy, 62
Metzger, Bruce Manning, 8, 108, 111, 115, 117, 121, 151
Micah, 26, 96, 109
Mickelsen, A. B., 56, 151
Microscope, 33
Migliore, D. L., 8
Military, 59

"Milky Way," 34
Miller, Donald G., 151
Miller, H. S., 125, 127, 128, 132, 151
Minstrel music, 25
Minuscule manuscripts, 112, 113, 117
Miracles, 28, 98
Modernizing Pentateuchal text, 49
Moffatt, James, 134
Möller, Wilhelm, 151
Moon, 34
"Morning star of the Reformation," 124
Mortality, Human, 38
Moses, 21, 25, 27, 34, 37, 40, 45, 49, 53, 68, 72, 76, 78, 85, 87, 89, 90, 92, 97, 104-106
Mount of transfiguration, 23
Murray, John, 7, 44, 45, 151
Myth, The term, 35, 36
Mythological literature, 35, 36

N

Nahum, 26
Nash, Ronald H., 152
Nathan the prophet, 18, 92
Nathanael, 72
Naturalistic assumptions, 29
Nature, "Vanity" of, 28
Nazareth, 85, 99, 100
Near East, 35, 46, 75
Nehemiah, 109
Neill, Stephen, 152
Neoorthodoxy, 7
Nestle, Eberhard, 115, 119
Nestle Greek New Testament, 116, 119
Netherlands, 59
"Neutral" New Testament text, 113
New birth, 18, 71, 78, 80
New covenant, 55, 67, 68
New English Bible, 136
New Testament built on O.T., 75
New Testament text, 111-121
New Testament's relation to O.T., 59, 60, 67-71, 75-77
Niebuhr, H. Richard, 152
Nineham, D. E., 152
Nineveh, 35
Nonresistance (See Agape love, Military, Warfare)
Normans, 122
Normative, Scripture as, 52
Numbers, Biblical, 33
Nygren, Anders, 152
NZR, 100

O

Oaths, 75

Obadiah, 26
Obedience of faith, 83, 84
"Occasional" elements in Scripture, 80, 81
Octapla, New Testament, 135
Old Latin manuscripts, 113
Old Testament's relation to N.T., 59, 60, 67-71, 75-77
Omega, 112, 118
Oral tradition of the Jews, 21, 22
Ordinances, N.T., 80
Origen, 113
Orlinsky, 110
Orm, 124
Ormulum, 124
Orr, James, 14, 39-41, 52, 152
Orthodoxy, 31
Ostraca, 111
Oxford University, 124, 126, 130, 131

P

Packer, J. I., 152
Palestine, 65
Papacy, 59
Papyrus and papyri, 112, 113, 117
Parables, 36, 37, 62, 101
Paradox, 32, 52
Paragraphing, 132
Parallel passages in O.T., 109
Parente, Pietro, 152
Parker, DeWitt H., 7
Parousia (Return) of Christ, 23, 79
Paschal lamb, 71
Passion Week, 100, 101
Patmos, 20
Patriarchal narratives, 30
Patrick, Saint, 123
Patton, Francis L., 152
Paul, 19, 23, 31, 37, 53, 55, 74, 77, 81, 87, 103
Payne, J. Barton, 152
Pekah's reign, Length of, 39
Pentateuch, 16, 27, 49, 128
Pentecost, 67, 72, 101
Perizzites, 49
Perry, C. M., 7
Persecution of dissenters, 69
Peter, 19, 23, 37, 74, 77, 80, 97, 102, 103
Pfeiffer, Robert H., 152
Pharaohs of Egypt, 15, 33, 89
Philemon, 37
Philip, 72, 74, 98
Philippians, 84
Philips, Dirk, 59
Philips, Obbe, 59
Philistines, 65
Picts, 122

Pilate, Pontius, 73, 102, 103
Pilgrim's Progress, 36
Pim, 66
Plagues in Egypt, 33, 90
"Plain sense" of Scripture, 57
Planets, 34
Plato, 13
Plenary inspiration, 52
Polygamy, 75
Polytheism, 35, 36
Prayer, 71
Predictive prophecy, 27
Presbyterians, 132
Preus, Robert D., 71, 152
Priesthood, O. T., 59, 87
Priestly code, 48
Princeton Theological Seminary, 7, 8, 133
Printing invented, in Europe, 126
Prophecy of Ahijah, 51
Prophetic interpretations, 26
Prophets, 16-18, 27, 32, 37, 40, 72, 74, 85
Prophets, Former, 16
Prophets, Latter, 16, 17
Prophets, Scrolls of, 16
Proverbs, 38
Providence of God, 71
Psalms, 18, 23, 24, 37, 86, 88, 101-104,
    107, 109, 124
Puritans, 130
Purvey, John, 125

Q

Queen Mary, 128, 129
"Queen of the Cursives," 113, 119
Quotation, Direct and indirect, 33

R

Rahner, Karl, S.J., 60, 152
Ramm, Bernard, 56, 152
Raphael, 137
Red Sea, 89
Redemption of Israel, 15, 88
Redemption of mankind, 87-105
Reformed Church, 60
Reformed Ecumenical Synod, 153
Reformers, 56-59
Regeneration (See New Birth)
Reid, J. K. S., 153
Reign of the Messiah, 90
Relation of the Testaments, 59, 67-71,
    75-77
Religious truth, Gen. 1 as, 35
Remnant saved, 71
Repentance, 79, 80
Reptiles, 35
"Rest," 24

Resurrection of Christ, 30, 101, 103-105,
    123
Return of Christ, 23, 42, 75, 102, 123
Reu, John M., 153
Reuchlin, 57
Revised Standard Version, 108, 119, 120,
    134-136
Revolt, Humans in, 14
Reynolds, Dr. John, 130
Rheims New Testament, 83, 130
Richardson, Alan, 153
Ridderbos, H. N., 153
Ridderbos, N. H., 153
Ridley, 129
Rieu, E. V., 137
"Right hand of God," 101
Riphath, 107
Ritschl, 24
Roberts, B. J., 109, 153
Robertson, E. H., 153
Robinson, H. Wheeler, 153
Robinson, James M., 56, 153
Rock badger ("coney"), 42
Rogers, John, 128, 129
Rolle, Richard, 124
Roman Catholicism, 59, 60, 136
Roman type, 129
Romans, Epistle to the, 23, 37, 80, 82, 83,
    87, 105, 137
Romans (people), 122, 123
Rome, 97
Rowley, H. H., 49, 153
Runia, Klaas, 153
Russia, 64, 65
Rust, Eric C., 154
Ryrie, Charles C., 154

S

Sabbath, 35
Sacramentalism, 81
Sacrifices, 59, 79, 87, 98
Saga, 36
Saint, 133
Saint Catherine's monastery, 116
Salvation, The Bible and, 34, 36, 43, 45-
    47, 53, 54, 70, 137
Samaritan Pentateuch, 106, 111
Samaritan woman, 96
Sampson, Thomas, 129
Samuel, Book of, 16, 28, 51, 65, 66, 107-
    109
Samuel the prophet, 15, 16, 18, 90, 102
Sasse, Hermann, 154
Satan, 91
Sattler, Michael, 59
Saul, 15, 16, 18, 65, 108, 109

Saxons, 122
Schaff, Philip, 133
Schrenk, Gottlob, 7
Scientific history, 39
Scientific precision, 39, 40
Scientific research, 33, 35, 39
Scots, 122
Scripture as God's Word, 21-25, 41
Scripture: Our sole source of theology, 36
Seamless robe, Christ's, 30
Second coming (See Return of Christ)
Second Esdras, 50
"Second Moses," 50
"Seed of Abraham," 14, 91
"Seed of David," 14, 92, 97, 103, 105
"Seed of the woman," 14, 15, 90, 91
"Seeing" Yahweh's message, 26
Sellars, Roy Wood, 7
Septuagint, 33, 40, 66, 106-109, 111, 134
Sermon on the Mount, 76
Servant of the Lord, 94, 95, 97
Shemaiah, 17
Sheol, 101
Shiloh, 17, 92
Simeon, 74, 99
Sin, 36
Sinai, Mt., 116
Sinaiticus manuscript, 113, 116
Sinner, Man addressed as, 34
Sinners, Christians as, 82, 83
Sins remitted, 99, 103, 104
Skeat, W. W., 125
Smart, James D., 56, 154
Smith, Miles, 131
Smith, Wilbur M., 58, 154
Smiths, 66
Snaith, Norman H., 154
Snyder, Graydon, 150
Society of Friends, 81
Sola scriptura, 60
Solar system, 34
Solomon, 15
Solomon's laver, 33
Son of David, 105
Son of God, 99, 105
Son of man, 96
Soncino Press, 110
Soteriological intent of Scripture, 34, 36, 43, 45-47, 52, 53, 70, 136
Source analysis of Hexateuch, 48
Sources used by Biblical writers, 43, 49, 50, 51
Souter, A., 112
Sovereignty of God, 35
Speeches, 33
State church, 59, 69

Stephanus, 115
Stevick, Daniel B., 154
Stonehouse, Ned B., 7, 154
"Strangers and pilgrims," 80
Style of individual writers, 51, 52
Sufficiency of the believer, 55, 56
Sun, 34, 35
Sussex, 122
Swift River, 126
Swiss Brethren, 69
Switzerland, 59
Sword of the Spirit, 19
Syllogism, 14, 41
Synecdoche, 62
Synoptic Gospels, 19, 30
Syntax, 62
Syria, 107, 112
Syriac Bible, 111
Syrian N.T. Greek text, 112

T

Tabernacle, 88
Tacitus, 111
Taverner, Richard, 128
Telescope, 33
Tenney, Merrill C., 154
Terry, M. S., 56, 154
Tertullian, 113
Teutons, 122
Text of Scripture, 106-121
Textual criticism, 106-121, 132
Textus receptus, 115, 118-121
Thayer, J. Henry, 133
Theocentric Account, 34
Theological assumptions, 29
Theological explanations, 36
Theological interpretation, 77-79
Theophany, 25
Thessalonians, 55
Thessalonica, 18
Thiele, Edwin R., 154
Thomas, John Newton, 154
Thompson, J. A., 154
"Three-decker universe," 46, 47
Throne of David, 92-94, 97, 99
Thummim, 109
Tiberias, 73
Timothy, 47, 56, 84
Tischendorf, C. von, 115, 116
Titus, 71
Todd, John M., 154
Torah, 28, 49
Tradition, 57-60, 83
Tropological interpretation, 57
Trustworthiness of Scripture, 41-50, especially 43, 44, 48

Twelve Minor Prophets, 16
Twilley, L. D., 154
Two-Sources Theory of Authority, 60
Tyndale, William, 126-129

U

Ultranationalism in Israel, 39
Unbelief, 24
Unchastity, 76
Uncial manuscripts, 111, 117
Unger, Merrill F., 154
Unicorn, 66
Union Theological Seminary, 134
Unitarian, 132
Unity of the Bible, 67, 70, 76, 77
University of Chicago, 7
University of Manchester, 8
University of Michigan, 7
University of the South, 134
Ur of the Chaldees, 49
Urim, 109
Ussher Chronology, 131
Uzzah, 18

V

Valen-Sendstad, Olav, 72
Van Til, Cornelius, 7, 154
Vanity of life without God, 38
Vaticanus manuscript, 113, 116
Verbal inspiration, 44, 51
Verduin, Leonard, 69
Verse division, 129
Vicarious suffering of the Messiah, 95, 97
Victory over sin, 83
Vilvorde Prison, 126
Vine, W. E., 155
Virgin birth of Christ, 98
Virgin Mary, 14, 98
Vischer, Wilhelm, 155
Vision of Isaiah, 51
Visions, 25, 26
Visions of Iddo, 51
Vocabulary and style, Individual, 52
Von Hofmann, J. C. K., 56
Vos, Johannes G., 155
Volgate (Latin) Version, 109, 111, 114, 124, 126, 134

W

"Waiting shelf," 71
Walvoord, John F., 44, 155
Warfare, 60, 69, 75
Warfield, B. B., 25, 52, 55, 155

Washing of the saints' feet, 80
Wealth, Man and, 38
Weights and measures, 33
Weigle, Luther A., 134
Weiss, Bernard, 115
Wellhausen, 30, 109
Wesley, John, 13
Wessex, 122
Westcott, B. F., 75, 113, 115, 116, 125-127
Westcott and Hort, 113, 116
Westermann, Claus, 155
Western N.T. Greek text, 113
Westminster, 130
Westminster Theological Seminary, 7, 8
Wettstein, J. J., 117
Whittingham, William, 129
Wild ox ("unicorn"), 66
Wilder, Amos N., 155
Wilson, Robert Dick, 155
Wine, 80
Wittenberg, 59
Woman's status in O.T., 75
Wood, James D., 56, 155
Woolley, Paul, 7, 8
Woolsey, T. D., 133
Word of God (Jesus Christ), 20, 21
Word of God (proclamation of Gospel), 18-20
Word of God (through prophets), 16-18
Word of God (written Scriptures), 21-25
Word of Yahweh, 16
Worms, Germany, 126
Wright, G. Ernest, 35, 155
"Writings" (Division III of Hebrew O.T.), 27
Württemberg Bible Society, 115
Wyclif, John, 58, 124-126

Y

Yahweh, 16-18
Yale University, 133, 134
Yoder, Edward, 7
Yoder, G. G., 8
Young, Edward J., 7, 155

Z

Zacharias, 99
Zechariah, 44, 97
Zedekiah, 27, 136
Zeugma, 63
Zimmerli, Walter, 7
Zophar, 64
Zürich Bible, 127
Zwingli, 56, 59

J. C. Wenger is Professor of Historical Theology in Goshen Biblical Seminary, a school of the Associated Mennonite Biblical Seminaries, Elkhart, Indiana. He has made a lifelong study of Anabaptism and has published numerous articles and books in the field.

He studied at Eastern Mennonite and Goshen colleges (BA), at Westminister and Princeton Theological seminaries, and at the universities of Basel, Chicago, Michigan (MA in philosophy), and Zurich (ThD).

He has taught at Eastern Mennonite and at Union Biblical (India) seminaries, and has served on the Committee on Bible Translation which prepared the *New International Bible*.

He is a member of the Evangelical Theological Society. He has served on the editorial boards of *Mennonite Quarterly Review, Studies in Anabaptist and Mennonite History,* and *The Mennonite Encyclopedia,* and on the executive council of the Institute of Mennonite Studies.

He has served the Mennonites as a deacon, a minister, and a bishop. He has been a member of their Historical Committee, Publication Board, Board of Education, district and general conference executive committees, and of the Presidium of the Mennonite World Conference.

He married the former Ruth D. Detweiler, RN, in 1937. They are the parents of two sons and two daughters.

The Conrad Grebel Lectures

The Conrad Grebel Lectureship was set up in 1950 to make possible an annual study by a Mennonite scholar of some topic of interest and value to the Mennonite Church and to other Christian people. It is administered by the Conrad Grebel Projects Committee appointed by and responsible to the Mennonite Board of Education. The committee appoints the lecturers, approves their subjects, counsels them during their studies, and arranges for the delivery of the lectures at one or more places.

The lectureship is financed by donors who contribute annually $500 each.

Conrad Grebel was an influential leader in the sixteenth-century Swiss Anabaptist movement and is honored as one of the founders of the Mennonite Church.

The lectures are published by Herald Press, Scottdale, Pa. 15683, and Kitchener, Ont. N2G 4M5, as soon as feasible after the delivery of the lectures. The date of publication by Herald Press is indicated by parenthesis.

Lectures thus far delivered are as follows:

1952—*Foundations of Christian Education*, by Paul Mininger.
1953—*The Challenge of Christian Stewardship* (1955), by Milo Kauffman.
1954—*The Way of the Cross in Human Relations* (1958), by Guy F. Hershberger.
1955—*The Alpha and the Omega* (1955), by Paul Erb.
1956—*The Nurture and Evangelism of Children* (1959), by Gideon G. Yoder.
1957—*The Holy Spirit and the Holy Life* (1959), by Chester K. Lehman.
1959—*The Church Apostolic* (1960), by J. D. Graber.
1960—*These Are My People* (1962), by Harold S. Bender.
1963—*Servant of God's Servants* (1964), by Paul M. Miller.

1969—*The Resurrected Life* (1965), by John R. Mumaw.

1965—*Creating Christian Personality* (1966), by A. Don Augsburger.

1966—*God's Word Written* (1966), by J. C. Wenger.

1967—*The Christian and Revolution* (1968), by Melvin Gingerich.

1968—*The Discerning Community: Church Renewal*, by J. Lawrence Burkholder.

1970—*Woman Liberated* (1971), by Lois Gunden Clemens.

1971—*Christianity and Culture: An African Context*, by Donald R. Jacobs.

1973—*In Praise of Leisure* (1974), by Harold D. Lehman.

1977—*Integrity: Let Your Yea Be Yea* (1978), by J. Daniel Hess.